Lecture Notes in Computer Science

Lecture Notes in Artificial Intelligence 16400

The series Lecture Notes in Artificial Intelligence (LNAI) was established in 1988 as a topical subseries of LNCS devoted to artificial intelligence.

The series publishes state-of-the-art research results at a high level. As with the LNCS mother series, the mission of the series is to serve the international R & D community by providing an invaluable service, mainly focused on the publication of conference and workshop proceedings and postproceedings.

Jawad Haqbeen · Rafik Hadfi · Takayuki Ito ·
Anastasija Nikiforova · Wenxin Li ·
Xingbo Wang · Yunlong Lu
Editors

Democracy and AI & Game AI Algorithms and Multi-Agent Learning

The 6th International Workshop on Democracy and AI, DemocrAI 2025
and the 2nd Workshop on Game AI Algorithms and Multi-Agent Learning, GAAMAL 2025
Held in Conjunction with IJCAI 2025
Montreal, QC, Canada, August 16–22, 2025
Proceedings

Editors
Jawad Haqbeen
Kyoto University
Kyoto City, Japan

Rafik Hadfi
Kyoto University
Kyoto City, Japan

Takayuki Ito
Kyoto University
Kyoto City, Japan

Anastasija Nikiforova
University of Tartu
Tartu, Estonia

Wenxin Li
Peking University
Beijing, China

Xingbo Wang
Peking University
Beijing, China

Yunlong Lu
Peking University
Beijing, China

ISSN 0302-9743 ISSN 1611-3349 (electronic)
Lecture Notes in Artificial Intelligence
ISBN 978-981-95-9666-9 ISBN 978-981-95-9667-6 (eBook)
https://doi.org/10.1007/978-981-95-9667-6

LNCS Sublibrary: SL7 – Artificial Intelligence

This Springer imprint is published by the registered company Springer Nature Singapore Pte Ltd.
The registered company address is: 152 Beach Road, #21-01/04 Gateway East, Singapore 189721, Singapore

Preface

The International Joint Conference on Artificial Intelligence (IJCAI) is a premier international gathering of researchers in AI. Since its founding in 1969, IJCAI has been the premier conference for the global AI community, fostering the exchange of groundbreaking advancements and achievements in artificial intelligence research.

This volume comprises the proceedings of two of the workshops of the 34th International Joint Conference on Artificial Intelligence (IJCAI), which took place in Montreal, Canada, from August 16 to August 22, 2025. It consists of the refereed and accepted papers from the 6th International Workshop on Democracy & AI (DemocrAI@IJCAI 2025) and the 2nd Workshop on Game AI Algorithms and Multi-Agent Learning (GAAMAL@IJCAI 2025).

A more detailed summary of two workshops is provided below.

In total, we received 24 submissions through the submission system. From these submissions, and after a double-blind review process, we accepted in total 8 papers for inclusion in this volume, 5 full and 3 short. Each paper was reviewed by at least 3 reviewers. We would like to thank the reviewers for both workshops for their contributions to this process.

We would like to thank the authors of all these submissions for their contributions.

January 2026

Jawad Haqbeen
Rafik Hadfi
Takayuki Ito
Anastasija Nikiforova
Wenxin Li
Xingbo Wang
Yunlong Lu

Preface

6th International Workshop on Democracy & AI (DemocrAI@IJCAI 2025)

We are pleased to present the proceedings of the 6th International Workshop on Democracy & AI (DemocrAI 2025), held in conjunction with the 34th International Joint Conference on Artificial Intelligence (IJCAI 2025) at Palais des congrès, Montreal, Canada, from August 16–22, 2025.

DemocrAI aims to bring together researchers and practitioners from machine learning, data science, political science, and related disciplines to explore how artificial intelligence can be applied to advance civic technologies and support democratic decision-making. DemocrAI 2025 provided an interdisciplinary forum to explore the current and future roles of AI in democratic systems. The workshop fostered critical dialogue among researchers and practitioners from artificial intelligence, political science, public policy, and the social sciences on how AI can be harnessed for democratic good, while carefully addressing its ethical, technical, and societal challenges.

The DemocrAI 2025 program featured two keynote talks, four invited lightning talks, three extended abstract presentations, and five full regular papers selected from 13 submissions. All submissions underwent a double-blind peer review process, with each paper receiving a minimum of three reviews.

We sincerely thank all authors for their valuable contributions, the reviewers for their careful and insightful evaluations, and the IJCAI 2025 organizers for their strong support. We also extend our appreciation to all participants for their active engagement.

August 2025

Jawad Haqbeen
Rafik Hadfi
Takayuki Ito
Anastasija Nikiforova

Keynotes

The Imperative for AI Literacy

By Mary Lou Maher, University of North Carolina at Charlotte, USA

Abstract: As Generative Artificial Intelligence (AI) becomes increasingly integrated into society and education, more institutions are implementing AI usage policies and offering introductory AI courses. These courses, however, should not replicate the technical focus typically found in AI courses. This presentation emphasizes the imperative for socio-technical AI literacy for an informed public, workforce, and AI professionals. AI literacy is framed as four mutually supporting pillars. These pillars encompass (1) understanding the scope and technical dimensions of AI technologies, (2) learning how to interact with (Generative) AI technologies, (3) applying principles of critical, ethical, and responsible AI usage, and (4) analyzing implications of AI on society. AI literacy is essential for all as society becomes increasingly affected by AI-powered technologies. Providing AI literacy education democratizes access to a critical understanding of the development, use, and impact of AI on society.

In Praise of Empathic AI: Can Empathic AI Increase Human Welfare?

By Michael Inzlicht, University of Toronto, Canada

Abstract: As loneliness rises and many people lack the emotional support they need, empathic AI may offer a surprising solution. This talk explores whether artificial agents can deliver empathy that rivals, or even exceeds, that of humans. Across multiple studies, we assess the quality of AI-generated empathy using both third-party evaluations and first-person experiences. Results reveal that AI can provide empathic responses comparable to humans, and is sometimes even preferred. Yet despite this promise, people often reject empathic AI. Part of this rejection is driven not by experience but by moralistic beliefs about what AI should or should not do. I suggest that while empathic AI has the potential to enhance human welfare, we must tread carefully—resisting both knee-jerk moral opposition and the temptation to outsource too much of our emotional lives to machines.

Invited Lighting Talks

Balancing Exploration and Exploitation in Immigration Selection: A Case for the Epsilon-Greedy Approach by Djalel Bouneffouf

Competitive Trap of AI Governance: How Can We Prevent Erosion of Human Wellbeing in the Age of Artificial General Intelligence? by Shun Shiramatsu

Algorithmic Modeling of the Rule of Law: Toward Democratic Accountability Through Simulation by Mohamed Ben Achour

A Study on Complex Matching of AI Agents Based on Designed Utility by Shun Okuhara, Takayuki Ito, and Gaozhi Xiao

Accepted Extended Abstracts

Democratizing and enhancing student participation in online education with LLM-based agents by Jawad Haqbeen, Sofia Sahab, and Takayuki Ito

An LLM-based Comparison of Social Choice Methods to Synthesize Human Preferences by Salim Hafid

Group Discussions Are More Positive with AI Facilitation: Evidence from VADER Sentiment Analysis by Sofia Sahab, Jawad Haqbeen, and Takayuki Ito

Organization

Organizing Chairs

Jawad Haqbeen	Kyoto University, Japan
Rafik Hadfi	Kyoto University, Japan
Takayuki Ito	Kyoto University, Japan
Anastasija Nikiforova	University of Tartu, Estonia

Technical Program Committee

Tomer Libal	University of Luxembourg, Luxembourg
Enrico Gerding	University of Southampton, UK
Uwe Serdült	University of Zurich, Switzerland & Ritsumeikan University, Japan
Sebastian Stein	University of Southampton, UK
Ming-Hung Wang	National Chung Cheng University, Taiwan
Rafael Mestre	University of Southampton, UK
Sofia Sahab	Kyoto University, Japan
Tomasz Janowski	Gdańsk University of Technology, Poland & University for Continuing Education Krems, Austria
Shichao Liu	Carleton University, Canada
Nina Rizun	Gdańsk University of Technology, Poland
David Duenas-Cid	Kozminski University, Poland
Shun Okuhara	Mie University, Japan
Mashrin Srivastava	Microsoft, USA
Magdalena Ciesielska	Gdańsk University of Technology, Poland
Guilherme Wiedenhoft	Universidade Federal do Rio Grande, Brazil

Preface

2nd Workshop on Game AI Algorithms and Multi-Agent Learning (GAAMAL@IJCAI 2025)

The Second Workshop on Game AI Algorithms and Multi-Agent Learning was held at Palais des congrès, Montreal, Canada on August 18th, 2025, in conjunction with the 34th International Joint Conference on Artificial Intelligence (IJCAI).

Games serve as sources of inspiration and open test-fields for human intelligence. Various games, ranging from traditional board games to video games and virtual reality games, have shared a history of evolution for more than 5000 years with civilization and the technology of human society. Games contain incarnations of diverse models in game theory and also provide rich simulations of real-world scenarios. In the present age, games continue to catalyze the development of artificial intelligence, proposing novel research problems and providing benchmarks for learning algorithms. To date, many games including Chess and Go have witnessed superhuman performance of AI algorithms, while human-level AI for more complicated games like Mahjong remains an open problem.

This workshop aimed to investigate specific solutions to different forms of games as well as general learning theories, frameworks, and methods for game playing and decision making. Invited speakers and presenters came from industry and academia, bringing diverse perspectives and experiences.

Authors were required to submit full-length manuscripts for single-blind peer review. A total of 12 submissions were reviewed by 10 experts in this field to guarantee each paper at least 3 reviewers. Based on the feedback, 3 selected papers (25%) were included in the volume published by Springer.

We thank the authors for submitting their excellent work, our reviewers for their timely and detailed reviews, our invited speakers, and all our attendees.

We sincerely hope their joint efforts will help advance this field and advocate for the research value of game AI.

January 2026

Wenxin Li
Xingbo Wang
Yunlong Lu

Organization

General Chair

Wenxin Li	Peking University, China

Program Committee Chairs

Wenxin Li	Peking University, China
Haifeng Zhang	Chinese Academy of Sciences, China
Weinan Zhang	Shanghai Jiao Tong University, China
Junliang Xing	Tsinghua University, China
Yunlong Lu	Peking University, China
Xingbo Wang	Peking University, China

Program Committee

Xiaotie Deng	Peking University, China
Yaodong Yang	Peking University, China
Xianping Tao	Nanjing University, China
Wenlong Li	Mahjong International League, Switzerland
Yutian Chen	Google DeepMind, UK
Lanzhou Zheng	WEIZHIYU (Beijing) Technology Co., Ltd., China
Haobo Fu	Tencent AI Lab, China

Contents

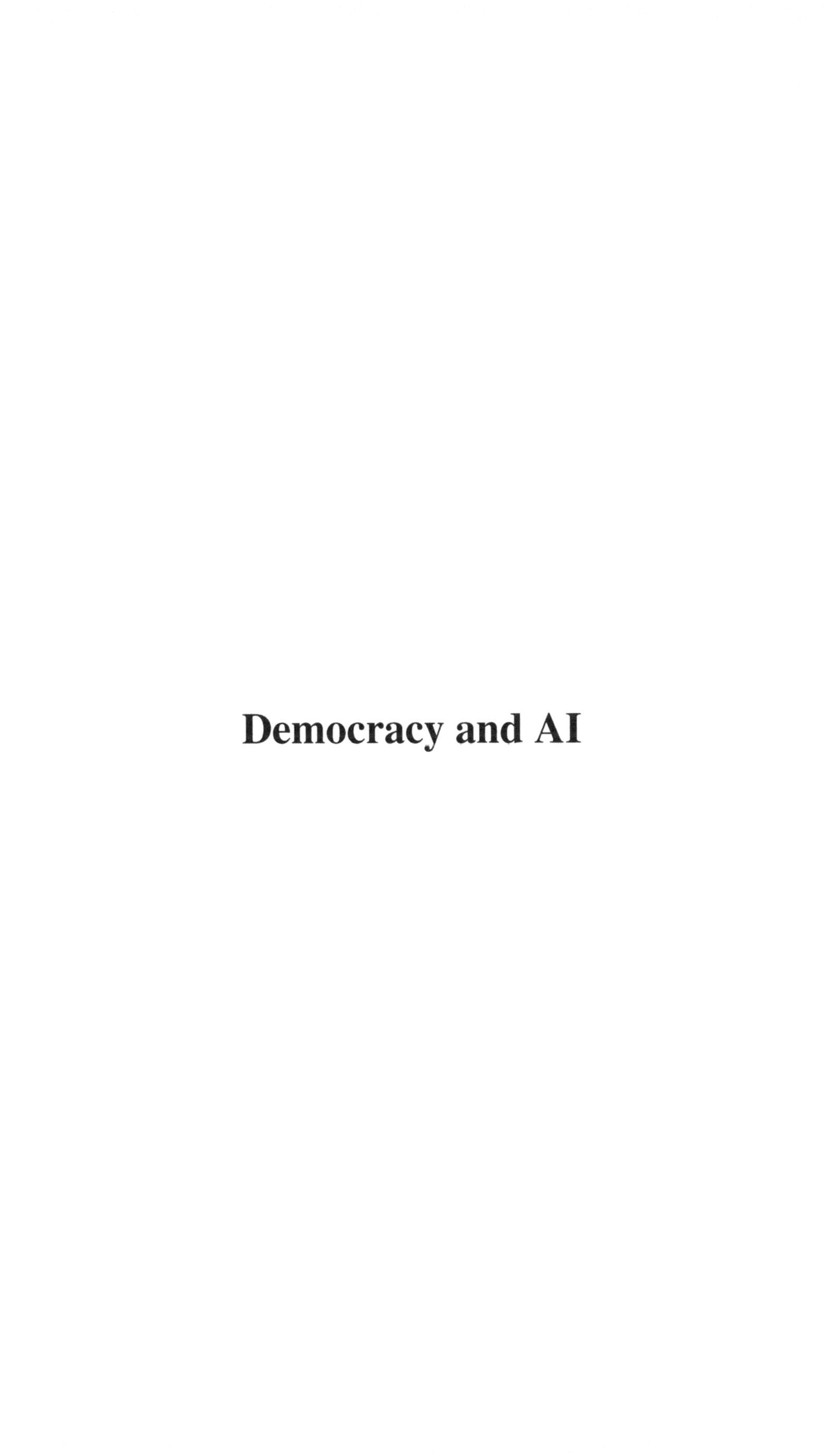

Democracy and AI

Deep Learning Based Multimodal Human Activity Recognition in Smart Homes Using SDHAR-HOME

Nowayer Alrashidi[1(✉)], Shichao Liu[1], Takayuki Ito[2], Jawad Haqbeen[2], and Alan Ruth[3]

[1] Carleton University, Ottawa, ON K1S 5B6, Canada
Nowayeralrashidi@cmail.carleton.ca, Shichaoliu@cunet.carleton.ca
[2] Kyoto University, Yoshida-Honmachi, Kyoto 606-8501, Japan
{ito,Jawad.haqbeen}@i.kyoto-u.ac.jp
[3] GRTHealth Inc., Aurora, ON L4G 0G9, Canada
Aruth@grthealth.com

Abstract. This paper presents a comparative analysis of two deep learning models, Bidirectional Recurrent Neural Networks (BiRNN) and a Self-Attention-based model, for multimodal Human Activity Recognition (HAR) using the SDHAR-HOME dataset. This real-world dataset captures diverse, non-intrusive sensor data, including motion, contact, temperature, humidity, vibration, ambient light, Bluetooth-based indoor positioning, and smart plug electricity consumption. By integrating appliance-level energy usage as a behavioral signal, the study introduces a novel privacy-conscious approach to activity recognition, offering an alternative to intrusive vision and audio-based systems. To classify complex and asynchronous activities, BiRNN is employed to capture bidirectional temporal dependencies, while a transformer-inspired Self-Attention model is implemented to attend selectively to the most informative temporal and sensor-specific features. The Self-Attention model outperforms BiRNN in weighted-average precision (User-1: 0.90; User 2: 0.82), recall (User-1: 0.77; User 2: 0.75), and F1-score (User-1: 0.83; User 2: 0.80), indicating a superior capability in classifying diverse activities. In contrast, the BiRNN model shows lower performance, particularly in weighted-average recall (User-1: 0.69; User 2: 0.70), and F1-score (User-1: 0.74; User 2: 0.73), due to its limited capacity to model long-range dependencies. This study introduces a benchmark framework that combines electric power data with environmental signals, contributing to the design of ethical, scalable HAR systems that respect user privacy, support aging-in-place, and enable equitable AI integration. The findings underscore that even limited appliance-level consumption data can be a valuable feature in multimodal HAR pipelines. By leveraging both temporal modeling and attention mechanisms, this work advances the development of responsible and privacy-aware activity recognition systems for smart home applications.

Keywords: Ambient Assisted Living · Bidirectional Recurrent Neural Network · Human Activity Recognition · Multimodal Sensor Data · Non-intrusive Load Monitoring · Self-Attention Mechanism · Smart Home

J. Haqbeen et al. (Eds.): IJCAI 2025, LNAI 16400, pp. 3–16, 2026.
https://doi.org/10.1007/978-981-95-9667-6_1

1 Introduction

Human Activity Recognition (HAR) has become a critical enabler for applications in healthcare monitoring, ambient assisted living (AAL), energy management, safety assurance, and real-time anomaly detection in both residential and industrial settings [1–4]. By interpreting multimodal sensor data to classify daily behaviors, HAR supports technologies that improve quality of life, optimize resource use, and enhance personal safety.

Despite its promise, most prior HAR research relies on intrusive sensing modalities such as vision-based systems [5, 6], ambient audio monitoring [7], or wearable devices [8]. These approaches face persistent challenges, including privacy risks, user compliance issues, and limited suitability for long-term deployment in multi-resident smart homes. This gap highlights the need for non-intrusive, scalable, and privacy-preserving HAR frameworks that can operate reliably in real-world residential environments.

To address this gap, the present study explores the SDHAR-HOME dataset, which integrates a diverse range of non-intrusive sensors including motion, contact, temperature, humidity, vibration, ambient light, Bluetooth-based positioning, and, importantly, smart plug-based appliance-level electricity consumption [9]. The integration of energy data provides a novel behavioral signal, enabling the recognition of subtle activity patterns through appliance usage, an aspect largely overlooked in prior work. Although the dataset contains both Bluetooth and wearable data for user differentiation, wearable streams were excluded to maintain strict non-intrusiveness.

This work introduces and evaluates two deep learning frameworks, a Bidirectional Recurrent Neural Network (BiRNN) and a Self-Attention model, marking their first application to the multimodal SDHAR-HOME dataset. While the BiRNN architecture models bidirectional temporal dependencies to capture sequential activity dynamics [10], the Self-Attention model, adapted from Mahmud et al. [11], leverages transformer encoders and global context pooling to learn long-range temporal and multimodal dependencies more effectively [12, 13]. A comparative evaluation of these two models provides critical insights into their respective strengths and limitations in multimodal HAR.

The core contributions of this paper are as follows:

- Highlighting the limitations of intrusive HAR approaches and motivating the need for privacy-preserving alternatives.
- Introducing appliance-level electricity consumption as a complementary non-intrusive signal for activity recognition.
- Evaluating BiRNN and Self-Attention architectures on the SDHAR-HOME dataset, demonstrating the advantages of attention mechanisms in capturing long-range dependencies.
- Establishing a baseline for integrating multimodal non-intrusive sensors with appliance-level data to advance scalable and ethical HAR systems.

2 Related Work

HAR has evolved through diverse sensing modalities, each offering unique strengths but also inherent limitations. Early efforts relied heavily on vision- and audio-based systems, which deliver high recognition accuracy but suffer from privacy concerns and sensitivity to environmental conditions [14]. Wearable-based approaches expanded HAR into healthcare and fitness domains, yet long-term compliance and user comfort remain persistent challenges. These limitations have motivated a shift toward non-intrusive sensing, where ambient and infrastructure-embedded devices such as motion, contact, and environmental sensors, enable activity recognition without compromising privacy. More recently, the incorporation of appliance-level energy consumption has emerged as a novel and underexplored signal, adding behavioral depth to non-intrusive HAR frameworks and setting the stage for this study [3, 4, 14–16].

Vision-based approaches remain one of the most widely studied in the HAR field. Leveraging deep convolutional and spatiotemporal neural networks, these systems can capture detailed movement patterns and achieve high accuracy in controlled settings [5, 6]. However, they are computationally expensive, highly sensitive to lighting and occlusion, and pose substantial privacy risks, making them unsuitable for continuous monitoring in private homes.

Another line of work has explored ambient audio to infer activities, often combined with vibration or environmental cues [7]. While audio sensors can capture subtle contextual signals such as cooking sounds or footsteps, they are inherently intrusive and prone to misclassification in noisy or multi-resident environments. Furthermore, microphones raise similar privacy and trust concerns as cameras, limiting their adoption in domestic settings.

Wearables such as accelerometers, gyroscopes, and physiological monitors have been extensively applied to HAR in domains like healthcare, rehabilitation, and fitness tracking [1, 2, 8]. These systems provide rich motion signals and have fueled advances in deep learning-based HAR, but their effectiveness relies on user compliance. Devices must be worn consistently and correctly, which is often impractical in real-world, multi-resident homes. This limits their scalability for long-term, unobtrusive monitoring.

To address these challenges, non-intrusive HAR has gained attention. Using ambient sensors such as motion detectors, door and window contacts, temperature, humidity, and light sensors, researchers have developed privacy-conscious frameworks for recognizing daily activities. These systems eliminate the need for cameras or wearables, making them more acceptable for long-term deployment in residential settings [3, 4]. While effective in preserving privacy, these systems often suffer from limited activity coverage and reduced discriminative power when activities produce overlapping sensor patterns. A particularly promising but underexplored dimension is the use of electricity consumption data for activity recognition. Appliance-level power signals reflect meaningful behavioral patterns, yet very few HAR frameworks have explicitly leveraged them. Ramos et al. [9] addressed this gap by releasing the SDHAR-HOME dataset, which uniquely combines ambient sensors with smart plug energy consumption, opening new opportunities for multimodal HAR. Despite these advances, the integration of appliance-level consumption data with deep learning for HAR remains largely unexamined. Building on these developments, the present work contributes to the emerging direction of non-intrusive HAR by evaluating two complementary deep learning architectures, BiRNN and Self-Attention, on the multimodal SDHAR-HOME dataset. By explicitly incorporating appliance-level electricity data alongside environmental signals, this study establishes a benchmark framework that highlights the added value of power consumption in improving recognition accuracy and advances the design of privacy-preserving and scalable HAR systems.

3 Methodology

3.1 Data Preparation and Preprocessing

a) *Data Preparation:*

A publicly available database, "Sensor Dataset for Human Activity Recognition at Home (SDHAR-Home)" developed by Raul Gomez Ramos, Jamie Duque Domingo, Eduardo Zalama, Jaime Gomez-Garcia-Bermejo, and Joaquin Lopez is used in this study [9]. This database consists of a variety of sensors strategically placed throughout a home occupied by 2 people and their pet, to detect and contextualize human activity in a 62-day period. These include motion sensors for presence detection, door/window sensors for object interaction, temperature and humidity sensors for activity context (e.g., cooking or showering), vibration sensors for furniture use, smart plugs for appliance monitoring (TV and washing machine), and light sensors to infer states like sleeping based on illumination conditions. The sensor data is annotated with activity labels, which represent 18 different types of daily routine activities which are watching TV, cooking, eating, relaxing, bathroom activity, dishwashing, showering, pet care, laundry, out of the home, taking medications, working, making simple food, dressing, chores, reading, sleeping and other (defines unlabeled activities) [9].

b) *Data Preprocessing:*

The following are applied on the SDHAR-Home Dataset [9]:

1. Temporal Sampling and Encoding: Standardized irregular sensor events using fixed time-interval sampling. Binary sensor outputs are converted to numerical 0 or 1. Appliance usage signals for the smart plugs encoded using zero-order hold technique.
2. Time-of-Day Feature Encoding: Time information transformed using normalized sine-cosine encoding to reflect cyclic daily patterns by applying Eqs. 1 and 2, where h is hour and m is minute.
3. Oversampling: Minority activity classes are oversampled to ensure uniform representation.
4. Data Sharing: Data-sharing mechanism between users for improving generalization on underrepresented activities.
5. Data Splitting: Assigning block-based stratification, where contiguous interval (blocks) of each labelled activity from the merged data is extracted. Post random shuffling of blocks, assignment of blocks go as follows, 70% to training, 10% to validation, and 20% to testing. This is done while warranting that no single activity

segment spans multiple sets. This process ensures realistic evaluation scenarios and efficient generalization of the model.

$$HourX = \cos\left(\frac{2\pi\left(h + \frac{min}{60}\right)}{24}\right) [9] \tag{1}$$

$$HourY = \sin\left(\frac{2\pi\left(h + \frac{min}{60}\right)}{24}\right) [9] \tag{2}$$

3.2 BiRNN Based Human Activity Recognition

The first proposed model for HAR based on BiRNN is designed to process the multimodal SDHAR-Home sensor data. The model is structured in multiple stages as each contributing to the effective extraction of temporal and contextual features to accurately classify activities performed by the residents within the household. The BiRNN HAR model architecture is displayed in Fig. 1 below,

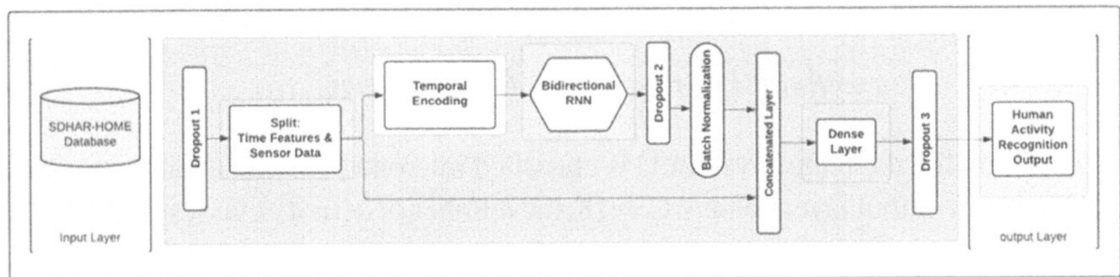

Fig. 1. BiRNN-based HAR model architecture showing preprocessing, temporal modeling using bidirectional RNNs, and final SoftMax classification

Step 1. The input data vector $x_{in} \in \mathbb{R}^D$ contains cyclic time encodings and flattened sensor readings. Where D is the dimensionality of the input feature vector (D = 2522). A dropout layer with a rate of 0.6 is applied to prevent overfitting,

$$\tilde{x} = Dropout_{0.6}(x\_in) \tag{3}$$

The regularized input is split into a time-encoding vector h ∈ ℝ2 capturing cyclic time information, and S ∈ ℝ^(D-2) representing sensor features.

Step 2. Sensor features s are reshaped into a temporal sequence S ∈ ℝ^(D-2) using a repeat operation, where,

$$w = \frac{(D-2)}{42} \tag{4}$$

The divisor 42 refers to the number of sensors features per timestep.

Step 4. The temporal sequence S is processed through a BiRNN compromised of 64 hidden units per direction. The hidden state h_t at timestep t in both forward and backward directions, and their concatenation are shown below,

$$\text{Forward}: \quad ht = ReLU\left(W_x S_t + W_h \vec{h}_{t-1} + b\right) [10,\ 13] \tag{5}$$

$$\text{Backward}: \quad \text{h}t = ReLU\left(W_x' S_t + W_h' \text{h}_{t+1} + b'\right) [10,\ 13] \tag{6}$$

$$\text{Concatenated Hidden States}: \quad r = [hw;\ hw], r \in \mathbb{R}\,128\ [10,\ 13] \tag{7}$$

Step 5. Following the BiRNN processing, the combined feature vector r undergoes a dropout regularization at a rate of 0.6 and a batch normalization,

$$Z = BatchNormalization(Dropout_{0 \cdot 6}(r)), z \in \mathbb{R}128 \tag{8}$$

Step 6. In this step feature fusion and expansion occurs, where the vector z is concatenated with the vector h, resulting in the following vector f,

$$f = [h;\ z], f \in \mathbb{R}130 \tag{9}$$

This is passed through a fully connected dense layer and a dropout layer,

$$u = ReLU\left(W_f f\right) \in \mathbb{R}^{8000}, \tilde{U} = Dropout_{0 \cdot 6}(u) \tag{10}$$

Step 7. Finally, the feature vector Ũ is classified into one of C human activity classes using a Softmax output layer. Where C = 18, the number of activity classes in the dataset,

$$y = Softmax\left(W_o \tilde{U}\right), y \in \mathbb{R}^c \tag{11}$$

3.3 Self-attention Based Human Activity Recognition

The proposed Self-Attention and global temporal attention model adapted from [11] is designed to enhance the capture of temporal and contextual dependencies across multimodal sensor inputs. The architecture is tailored to the SDHAR-HOME dataset and follows a structured pipeline as depicted in Fig. 2 below,

Step 1. The input to the model is a flattened feature vector x_flat ∈ ℝ^ (2522), consisting of cyclic time features and sensor readings. The first two cyclic time features are removed using a Lambda operation to isolate the sensor-specific features,

$$X\_sens = Lambda(x\_flat)[:, 2:] \in \mathbb{R}^{(2520)} \tag{12}$$

Step 2. The resulting vector is reshaped into a time-series tensor X ∈ ℝ^ (60 x 42), enabling temporal alignment of sensor features. A 2D convolution is applied across the input to compute intra-sensor attention logits q = Conv2D(X) to capture varying contributions across modalities. These are normalized using a SoftMax function to obtain attention weights over sensor modality k at timestep i as shown in Eq. 16 below,

$$a_{i,k} = \frac{exp\left(q_{i,k}\right)}{\sum_{j=1}^{F} exp\left(q_{i,j}\right)} [11] \tag{13}$$

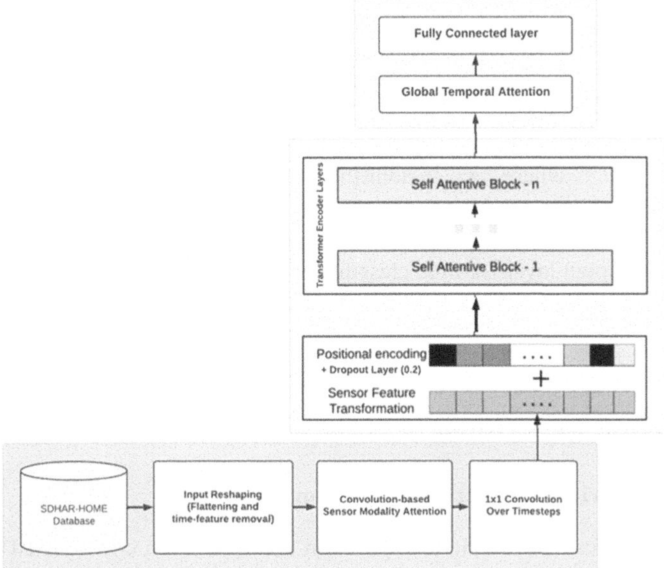

Fig. 2. Self-Attention-based HAR model architecture using transformer encoders and temporal attention to classify activities from SDHAR-HOME [11]

Step 3. The attention-weighted sensor output is passed through a 1 x 1 Conv1D operation with ReLU activation and augmented with positional encoding as shown in Eq. 17 and 18 below,

$$P = ReLU(Conv1D_{128}(S)) \in \mathbb{R}^{60X\,128} \tag{14}$$

$$P' = Dropout_{0.2}(P + \frac{PE(P)}{\sqrt{128}}) \in \mathbb{R}^{60X\,128} \tag{15}$$

Step 4. The encoded input is passed through two stacked transformer encoder layers. Here, multi-headed Self-Attention are employed to capture long-range dependencies,

$$f_{sa}^{(hj)}(q, k, v) = softmax\left(\frac{q.k^T}{\sqrt{d_k}}\right)v \text{ [11]} \tag{16}$$

The multi-head Self-Attention mechanism is defined as,

$$s_{mha} = W_o \cdot \text{concat}\left(f_{sa}^{(h1)}, \ldots\ldots\ldots\ldots, f_{sa}^{(h_{n-1})}, f_{sa}^{(h_n)}\right) \text{ [11]} \tag{17}$$

Step 5. A global temporal attention mechanism aggregates the temporal features into a single context vector,

$$c_i = \sum_t a^{(ti)} s^{(ti)}, a^{(ti)} = \frac{\exp\left(\left(g^{(ti)}\right)^T \cdot g_s\right)}{\sum_t \exp\left(g^{(ti)} g_s\right)} \text{ [11]} \tag{18}$$

$$\text{where, } g^{(ti)} = \tanh\left(W_{ga} \cdot s^{(ti)} + b_{ga}\right) \text{ [11]} \tag{19}$$

Step 6. The context vector c ∈ ℝ^128 is passed through a fully connected layer followed by a dropout layer for final classification,

$$\hat{y} = \text{Softmax}\left(W_2 \cdot Dropout_{0.2}(\text{ReLU}(W_1 \cdot \text{ c} + b_1)) + b_2\right) \in \mathbb{R}^{18} \tag{20}$$

4 Results and Evaluations

4.1 Human Activity Recognition Evaluation Metrics

This section outlines the training configuration and evaluation criteria used to develop and assess the BiRNN and Self-Attention-based models for HAR. The selected hyper-parameters were optimized to ensure stable convergence and generalization across users in the SDHAR-HOME dataset (Table 1).

Table 1. Hyperparameters for training the BiRNN and Self-Attention HAR model

	Hyperparameter Values	
Hyperparameter Type	BiRNN	Self-Attention
Optimizer	Adam Optimizer, learning rate = 1 x 10^{-5}, learning rate decay = 1 x 10^{-6}	Adam Optimizer, learning rate = 1 x 10^{-3}
Loss	Sparse categorical cross entropy	Sparse categorical cross entropy
Batch size	128	128
Early stopping	Patience = 10 (monitored on val_loss)	Patience = 10 (monitored on val_loss)
Model Checkpoint	Based on val_accuracy	Based on val_accuracy
Dropout	Dropout rate = 0.6	Dropout rate = 0.2
Epochs	Up to 200	Up to 200

To assess model performance, four primary classification metrics were employed, accuracy, precision, recall, and F1-score. These metrics are derived from the fundamental classification outcomes per class *i*: True Positives (TPi) are instances correctly classified as class i; False Positives (FPi) are instances from other classes that were incorrectly labeled as class i; False Negatives (FNi) are instances of class i that were misclassified as a different class; and True Negatives (TNi) are instances from all other classes that were correctly not classified as class i. The corresponding metric definitions are shown in Eqs. 21 – 24.

$$\text{Accuracy metric, } Accuracy_i = \frac{\mathrm{TP}_i + \mathrm{TN}_i}{\mathrm{TP}_i + \mathrm{TN}_i + \mathrm{FP}_i + \mathrm{FN}_i} [17] \quad (21)$$

$$\text{Precision metric, } Precision_i = \frac{\mathrm{TP}_i}{\mathrm{TP}_i + \mathrm{FP}_i} [17] \quad (22)$$

$$\text{Recall metric, } Recall_i = \frac{\mathrm{TP}_i}{\mathrm{TP}_i + \mathrm{FN}_i} [17] \quad (23)$$

$$\mathrm{F1} - \text{score metric, } f1 = \frac{2(TPi + FPi) + (TPi + FNi)}{TPi} [17] \quad (24)$$

$$Supporti = TPi + FNi \quad (25)$$

To evaluate model performance across multiple classes, aggregate metrics are used:

$$\text{Macro} - \text{averaging, Macro} - \text{Metric} = \frac{1}{C} \cdot \sum \mathrm{Metric}_i \quad (26)$$

$$\text{Weighted} - \text{averaging, Weighted} - \text{Metric} = \frac{\sum \mathrm{Support}_i \cdot \mathrm{Metric}_i}{\sum \mathrm{Support}_i} \quad (27)$$

4.2 Comparative Analysis of HAR Model Architectures

Table 2. Performance Metrics Results for BiRNN and Self-Attention HAR Models

User	Performance Metrics	BiRNN		Self-Attention	
		Macro Average	Weighted Average	Macro Average	Weighted Average
User-1	Precision	0.49	0.86	**0.60**	**0.90**
	Recall	0.58	0.69	**0.64**	**0.77**
	F1-Score	0.47	0.74	**0.57**	**0.83**
	Accuracy	0.93	0.90	**0.95**	**0.91**
User-2	Precision	0.36	0.79	**0.44**	**0.82**
	Recall	0.39	0.70	**0.51**	**0.75**
	F1-Score	0.35	0.73	**0.44**	**0.80**
	Accuracy	0.94	0.90	**0.96**	**0.91**

Table 2 summarizes the comparative performance of BiRNN and Self-Attention-based models for multimodal HAR using the SDHAR-HOME dataset. The Self-Attention model consistently outperforms BiRNN across all key performance metrics, achieving higher weighted-average precision (User-1: 0.90; User-2: 0.82), recall (User-1: 0.77; User 2: 0.75), F1-score (User-1: 0.83; User 2: 0.80) and accuracy (User-1: 0.91; User-2: 0.91).

A per-activity analysis indicated stronger performance for tasks associated with appliances, such as watching TV and laundry. Activities with fewer samples or overlapping sensor signals, such as pet care and medication intake, showed weaker classification results.

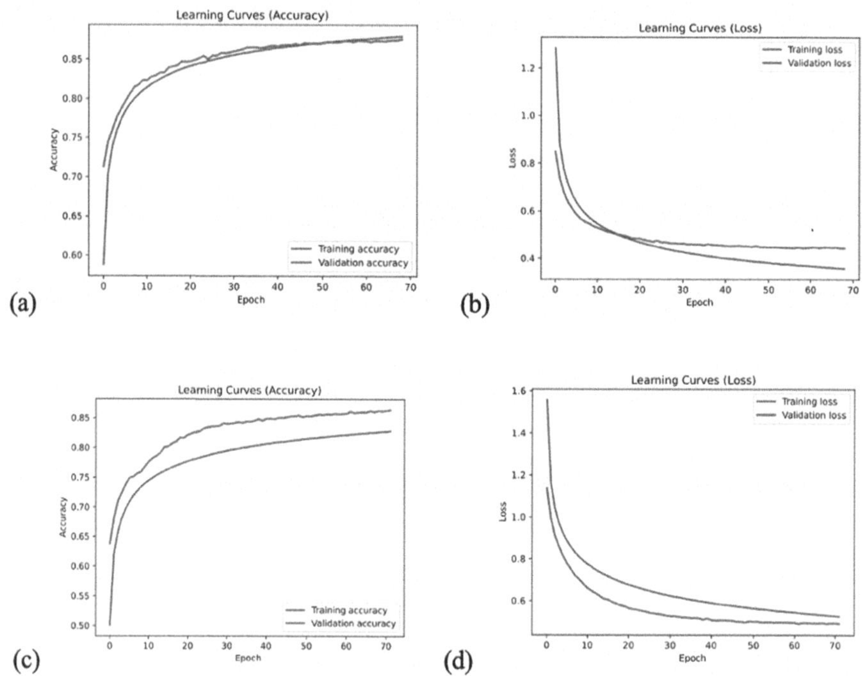

Fig. 3. Neural network training graphs for user 1 and 2. (a) BiRNN Accuracy User-1, (b) BiRNN Loss User-1, (c) BiRNN Accuracy User-2, (d) BiRNN Loss User-2

The learning curves in Fig. 3 show that the BiRNN model converged gradually, reaching final validation accuracy of approximately 85% for User-1 and 80% for User-2. As shown in Fig. 4, the Self-Attention model reached over 95% training accuracy within 20 epochs and stabilized between 90–95% validation accuracy. The curves also suggest mild overfitting for User-1 in the Self-Attention model.

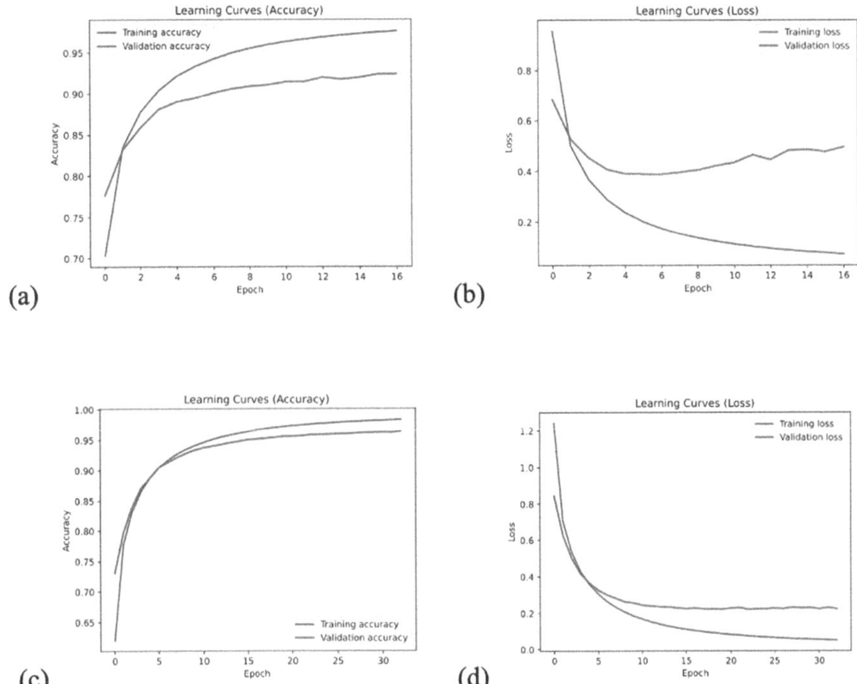

Fig. 4. Neural network training graphs for user 1 and 2. (a) Self-Attention Accuracy User-1, (b) Self-Attention Loss User-1, (c) Self-Attention Accuracy User-2, (d) Self-Attention Loss User-2

5 Discussion

The comparative evaluation indicates that the Self-Attention model provides more robust performance than the BiRNN across both users. Its higher weighted-average precision, recall, and F1-scores reflect the benefits of attention mechanisms in handling multimodal HAR data. This is consistent with prior work on transformer-inspired architectures [11, 12], which demonstrated that self-attention effectively captures long-range dependencies and selectively emphasizes informative sensor features. In contrast, the BiRNN model, while competent at modeling sequential dependencies, showed limitations in capturing broader temporal and contextual relationships. Its lower macro-average metrics suggest difficulty in distinguishing complex or overlapping activities. This observation is consistent with earlier findings that recurrent models are prone to performance degradation when activity distributions are imbalanced or when dependencies extend across long time spans [10, 13].

The results also reveal the impact of dataset imbalance. Activities such as watching TV and laundry were classified with higher accuracy, as they are strongly characterized by distinct appliance usage patterns and motion signals. In contrast, less frequent or overlapping activities, such as pet care and medication intake, showed weaker performance. This highlights the challenge of real-world HAR, where activity distributions are rarely uniform. Future work could address this issue through cost-sensitive learning, advanced resampling strategies, or activity-specific loss functions.

The training dynamics further illustrate the trade-offs between the two models. The Self-Attention model converged faster and achieved higher validation accuracy but exhibited mild overfitting, particularly for User-1. This suggests that while attention-based models are powerful, they may require stronger regularization or larger datasets to generalize effectively. Hybrid architectures that combine recurrent and attention layers could balance the strengths of both approaches by capturing local dependencies while retaining the ability to model global context.

Overall, the findings support the potential of integrating appliance-level energy consumption into HAR pipelines, as activities tied to appliance usage showed stronger recognition accuracy. The results also reaffirm the effectiveness of attention-based mechanisms in multimodal, non-intrusive HAR. At the same time, they highlight ongoing challenges related to dataset imbalance, generalization, and interpretability. Addressing these issues will be critical for developing scalable, privacy-preserving HAR systems that can function reliably in real-world, multi-resident smart homes.

6 Conclusion

This study addresses the challenge of recognizing human activities in smart homes by comparatively evaluating two deep learning architectures, BiRNN and Self-Attention, on the multimodal SDHAR-HOME dataset. The integration of diverse sensor data, including motion, temperature, humidity, vibration, ambient light, Bluetooth-based positioning, and electricity consumption, represents an advancement beyond conventional intrusive HAR approaches. Appliance-level signals enriched contextual understanding of daily activities, improving classification accuracy and practicality in real-world scenarios. The Self-Attention model consistently outperformed BiRNN across precision, recall, and F1-score, particularly in modeling long-range dependencies and asynchronous activities. In contrast, BiRNN was better suited for local patterns but less effective for complex or infrequent activities. Both models were impacted by dataset imbalance, with stronger performance on appliance-driven tasks such as watching TV and laundry, and weaker results for less frequent activities such as pet care and medication intake. These findings highlight the value of incorporating energy consumption data into HAR pipelines while underscoring the importance of addressing imbalance and generalization challenges.

This research establishes a benchmark framework that supports scalable, ethically aligned HAR systems, with relevance to AAL, eldercare, and sustainable smart home design. Future work should focus on hybrid attention–recurrent models, domain adaptation strategies, and the use of more diverse datasets with balanced activity distributions. Improving model interpretability and incorporating user feedback mechanisms will also be critical for building transparency and trust. By advancing HAR with non-intrusive and ethically aligned sensing, this study contributes to the development of responsible AI systems that support residents while safeguarding privacy in everyday living environments.

Acknowledgments. This study was funded by National research Council of Canada Grant Aging in Place (AiP-303-1).

Disclosure of Interests. The authors have no competing interests to declare that are relevant to the content of this article.

References

1. Lara, O.D., Labrador, M.A.: A survey on human activity recognition using wearable sensors. IEEE Commun. Surv. Tutorials. **15**, 1192–1209 (2013). https://doi.org/10.1109/surv.2012.110112.00192
2. Nweke, H.F., Teh, Y.W., Al-garadi, M.A., Alo, U.R.: Deep learning algorithms for human activity recognition using mobile and wearable sensor networks: state of the art and research challenges. Expert Syst. Appl. **105**, 233–261 (2018). https://doi.org/10.1016/j.eswa.2018.03.056
3. Ravuri, A., et al.: A systematic literature review on human activity recognition. J. Electr. Syst. **20**, 1175–1191 (2024). https://doi.org/10.52783/jes.2848
4. Sedaghati, N., Ardebili, S., Ghaffari, A.: Application of human activity/action recognition: a review. Multimedia Tools Appl. (2025). https://doi.org/10.1007/s11042-024-20576-2
5. Beddiar, D.R., Nini, B., Sabokrou, M., Hadid, A.: Vision-based human activity recognition: a survey. Multimedia Tools Appl. **79**, 30509–30555 (2020). https://doi.org/10.1007/s11042-020-09004-3
6. Bhola, G., Dinesh Kumar Vishwakarma: A review of vision-based indoor HAR: state-of-the-art, challenges, and future prospects. Multimedia Tools and Applications. 83, (2023). https://doi.org/10.1007/s11042-023-15443-5
7. Koch, M., Pfitzinger, T., Schlenke, F., Kohlmorgen, F., Groll, R., Wöhrle, H.: Recognition of human activities based on ambient audio and vibration data. IEEE Access. **12**, 174399–174412 (2024). https://doi.org/10.1109/access.2024.3457912
8. De Leonardis, G., et al.: Human activity recognition by wearable sensors: comparison of different classifiers for real-time applications. In: 2018 IEEE International Symposium on Medical Measurements and Applications (MeMeA) (2018). https://doi.org/10.1109/memea.2018.8438750
9. Ramos, R.G., Domingo, J.D., Zalama, E., Gómez-García-Bermejo, J., López, J.: SDHAR-HOME: a sensor dataset for human activity recognition at home. Sensors. **22**, 8109 (2022). https://doi.org/10.3390/s22218109
10. Schuster, M., Paliwal, K.K.: Bidirectional recurrent neural networks. IEEE Trans. Signal Process. **45**, 2673–2681 (1997). https://doi.org/10.1109/78.650093
11. Mahmud, S., et al: Human activity recognition from wearable sensor data using self-attention. https://arxiv.org/abs/2003.09018. Accessed 28 Jan 2025
12. Vaswani, A., et al.: Attention is all you need (2017)
13. Berglund, M., Raiko, T., Honkala, M., Kärkkäinen, L., Vetek, Á., Karhunen, J.: Bidirectional recurrent neural networks as generative models. In: The 29th International Conference on Neural Information Processing Systems. **1**, 856–864 (2015)
14. Arshad, M.H., Bilal, M., Gani, A.: Human activity recognition: review, taxonomy and open challenges. Sensors. **22**, 6463 (2022). https://doi.org/10.3390/s22176463
15. Islam, Md.M., Nooruddin, S., Karray, F., Muhammad, G.: Human activity recognition using tools of convolutional neural networks: a state of the art review, data sets, challenges, and future prospects. Comput. Biol. Med. **149**, 106060 (2022). https://doi.org/10.1016/j.compbiomed.2022.106060

16. Jiang, J., Kong, Q., Plumbley, M.D., Gilbert, N., Hoogendoorn, M., Roijers, D.M.: Deep learning-based energy disaggregation and On/off detection of household appliances. ACM Trans. Knowl. Discov. Data **15**, 1–21 (2021). https://doi.org/10.1145/3441300
17. Tam, S., Said, R.B., Tanriover, O.O.: A ConvBiLSTM deep learning model-based approach for twitter sentiment classification. IEEE Access. **9**, 41283–41293 (2021). https://doi.org/10.1109/access.2021.3064830

Finding Our Moral Values: Guidelines for Value System Aggregation

Víctor Abia Alonso[1(✉)], Marc Serramia[2], and Eduardo Alonso[1]

[1] City St George's, University of London, London, UK
victor.abia-alonso@citystgeorges.ac.uk
[2] IIIA - CSIC, Barcelona, Spain

Abstract. Ensuring AI aligns with our moral values is an important problem. To achieve AI alignment though, we first need to know what values we want AI to align with. However, obtaining a model of society's values is far from a simple problem. This problem, called value inference, typically needs to perform *value system aggregation* which consists in combining moral value models of several individuals to obtain one representing everybody. So far, only one such method has been proposed. This paper discusses why research in value system aggregation is necessary and outlines avenues to implement it depending on the value alignment problem at hand. In particular, we discuss how value system aggregation can be useful for policymaking applications.

Keywords: Value alignment · Aggregation · Participatory Budgets

1 Introduction

Ensuring AI aligns with our moral values is one of the key challenges for AI research in the coming years. However, obtaining the value system (i.e. the moral values and value preferences) we want AI to align with is an important preliminary step often overlooked. The process of obtaining a societal value system is not only useful for AI alignment but for other areas like governance and policymaking. Institutions like the European Commission highlight the importance of moral values to better understand citizens, co-create, and communicate policy [28]. Thus, in the case of policymaking, a model of citizen values would be useful both to inform governments and to use it in AI tools for policymaking.

Researchers have only very recently started to look into value inference, with Liscio et al. [17] presenting an approach based on three steps: value identification, value system estimation, and value system aggregation. Value identification is concerned with identifying the moral values that are relevant for a context (e.g. if we want to discuss traffic planning the value of security is relevant whereas the value of tradition is not relevant). Value system estimation is the process of eliciting the value system (that is the set of moral values and their preferences) of an individual citizen. Finally, value system aggregation consists in combining the values of all citizens into a common representation of all society. While there have been multiple proposals in value identification (e.g. [18,37]) and in value

J. Haqbeen et al. (Eds.): IJCAI 2025, LNAI 16400, pp. 17–27, 2026.
https://doi.org/10.1007/978-981-95-9667-6_2

system estimation (e.g. [1,33]), there has been only one proposed approach to value system aggregation [16]. Furthermore, the authors of this method did not study the ethical properties or describe the use cases for which it is better suited.

This paper aims to explore ideas for possible paths to value system aggregation. In more detail, this paper provides a taxonomy of value system aggregation approaches based on four key dimensions: judgment structure, ethical paradigms of aggregation, generality, and deliberation. Furthermore, we provide an exploration of practical use cases illustrating how different aggregation approaches can address value alignment challenges in policymaking.

2 Motivation: Participatory Budgets

Participatory democracy serves as an alternative to representative democracy allowing citizens to get involved in day-to-day policymaking. Although there are many forms of participatory methods, like parliamentary petitioning [23,24], in this section we focus on participatory budgets (PBs).

PBs allow residents to make proposals to spend a pre-defined budget. Then, citizens vote on the proposals they like most and a resource allocation process selects the proposals which get funded (usually considering votes only). The *Participatory Budget World Atlas* counts more than 10,000 participatory budgeting processes worldwide in 2021. Despite their popularity, PBs suffer from relatively low participation, for example, the Paris PB process (considered one of the most successful) in its 2023 iteration attracted 137.622 voters, which represents about 6.5 % of residents [22]. Furthermore, empirical studies have found low participation leads to bias in the result benefitting wealthier citizens [27]. Consequently, results in PB processes may fail to reflect the priorities of all the population. Given that the approved projects will affect all citizens, it would be desirable to consider votes while also consider the preferences of all citizens (thus correcting the biases of the voter base).

In practice, **value-system aggregation** can be used to find a representation of the society's values. These values can then be considered in the resource allocation process to compensate for the voter bias due to low participation. Serramia et al. [31] show how to find a compromise PB allocation considering both the votes of participants and societal values. Importantly, the authors show with real world data that this compromise solution highly satisfies both participant and non-participant citizens. This shows the usefulness of societal values in AI-aided policymaking applications to increase democratic quality. Hereafter we will use participatory budget allocation as the base example for the different approaches to value system aggregation we discuss.

3 Background: Value Systems

Context. In applied ethics [2,26], reasoning the goodness of actions and decisions with values is dependent on the *context*. This prevails in the AI value alignment literature [18,21,32] and thus, for value-guided decision and policy making. For example, if we want to increase welfare in a society with older citizens we might want to invest more in healthcare than in education, whereas in a younger society the reverse might be best. In practice, we can represent contexts in a computer-readable way using any logical language.

Values. A *value* is a deeply held belief that guides decision-making by defining what is important and desirable [29]. We formally characterize values as utility functions that assess the desirability of actions. Given an action a and a context c, each value v is defined by two judgment functions: $v^+(a, c)$ evaluates how good or bad is performing a in the context, while $v^-(a, c)$ evaluates how good or bad is avoiding to perform a in that context. The functions output a number in $[-1, 1]$. For instance, in a traffic-accident context the value *benevolence* rates the action HELP positively ($v^+(help, accident) = 1$) while avoiding to perform this action is negatively judged ($v^-(help, accident) = -1$).

Value Systems. When making value-aligned decisions we will usually consider more than one value. Naturally, with several values, we may have preferences between them. We formalise these values and preferences as a *value system* which is a pair $VS = \langle V, \succcurlyeq \rangle$ where V is a set of values and $\succcurlyeq$ preferences among them.

Value System Aggregation. Given the set of all possible value systems $\mathcal{VS}$, a *value-system aggregation function* is a mapping $F : \mathcal{VS}^n \rightarrow \mathcal{VS}$ that receives n citizen value systems and returns the consensus one. Importantly, although preference aggregation is a well-studied problem in the social choice literature, it cannot be readily applied to value system aggregation, this is for two reasons. First, typical preference aggregation treats options as atomic, whereas in value system aggregation must consider the structure of judgement functions. Second, while preference aggregation emphasises classical social-choice axioms (e.g. monotonicity, independence of irrelevant alternatives), value-system aggregation prioritises ethical properties and application-specific design criteria.

4 Personal Vs. Universal Judgements

A fundamental consideration when designing a value system aggregation approach is whether all agents share a common understanding of the values (i.e. their judgement functions). If interpretations vary, the aggregation process must reconcile these differences by establishing a consensus interpretation for each value along with the collective preferences. Conversely, if universal judgements are assumed, the aggregation process is simplified in this regard, as the structure of values remains consistent throughout. Next, we discuss each case in more detail and explain its use cases.

Personal judgements. People usually have different understandings of a value, for example, many people associate the value of security with gun control, while others associate security to being able to defend themselves with guns. If we allow personal judgements, we allow that the value systems to aggregate may contain different understandings of the same value. In this case, the aggregation of the value systems has to be able to aggregate these judgements apart from the preferences.

Use Case 1. Aggregation approaches considering personal judgements are useful in cases where the agents have small differences in their understanding of how values judge actions but do not hold opposite views. Otherwise, the aggregated value judgements may not be shared by anybody. In cases with opposed views it may be better to reconcile them before aggregation.

Universal judgements. This option assumes every value system to be aggregated shares the same judgement functions for its values. For example, if we are making decisions in the traffic context, the value of security will almost universally be linked to the probability of having an accident, there is no room for different interpretations, thus in this case we could assume a universal understanding. Note that, universal judgements eases aggregation (as only preferences have to be aggregated) but may flatten moral nuance.

Use Case 2. Domains in which there is no room for interpretation of values or policy domains with polarised interpretations (pro- vs anti-gun) where differences are so large that in order for the aggregation to make sense agree on a common definition, as summarized in Table 1.

Table 1. Comparison of Universal and Individual Value Approaches.

	Universal judgements	**Individual judgements**
Representation	May not capture all perspectives.	Custom interpretations; diverse perspectives.
Comparability	Preferences directly comparable.	Preferences not directly comparable.
Value Identification	Hard. People may not share the assumed universal judgement.	Easy. Everyone can use their own judgment.
Value Estimation	Easy. Estimate preferences only.	Hard. Estimate preferences and judgments.
Consensus Output	Clear, interpretable consensus value system.	Value judgements may lose meaning.

Compromise Strategies. On the one hand, if the big differences among agents prevent a meaningful consensus, aggregation could focus not on a single output, but rather on first clustering similar value interpretations and then output several possible consensus that preserve the individual interpretations of values. On the other hand, to make shared value judgements more nuanced, value identification could adopt a more exhaustive approach—distinguishing between different interpretations of a value as distinct values themselves. For instance, following on the previous example on guns and the value of security, rather than treating "security" as a single value with multiple interpretations, one might identify "personal security" and "public security" as separate, clearly defined values. This way people in favour of gun regulation would prefer "public security" over "personal security", while the inverse would be true for those in favour of gun ownership. This emphasis on granular value identification illustrates how value system aggregation should inform value estimation, supporting the view that the interaction between value inference steps remains an under-explored yet crucial area of research [17]. Additionally, deliberation between agents may lead to meta-agreements on the concepts being used, which, as discussed in Sect. 7, aligns with the universal judgement approach.

5 Aggregation Ethical Paradigms

Beyond value judgement choices, the aggregation process may follow different aggregation principles (e.g. fairness). Distance-based aggregation is a widely used aggregation framework [3] that selects the consensus that minimises total distance to all inputs. Thus, given a set of candidate options C, a set of agents $1, \ldots, n$, preference orders $\succeq_i$ for each agent i over C, and a distance function d between preference orders, a consensus order can be found using the general distance-based aggregation formula 1:

$$\succeq_{\text{agg}} = \arg\min_{\succeq} \sum_{i=1}^{n} d(\succeq, \succeq_i) \quad (1) \qquad vs_{\text{agg}} = \arg\min_{vs \in \mathcal{VS}} \Big(\sum_{i=1}^{n} d(vs, vs_i)^p \Big)^{1/p} \quad (2)$$

A classic example in social choice is the Kemeny rule which minimizes Kendall's tau distance [14]. Distance-based aggregation have been studied by the work of Gonzalez-Pachón et al. [9] which employs the p-metric distance function to categorize guiding ethical principles; this can be generalised to value system aggregation. Thus, given agents $1, \ldots, n$, a value system vs_i for each agent i, a distance function d between value systems, and let $\mathcal{VS}$ be the set of all possible value systems, we can then define distance-based value system aggregation incorporating the ethical parameter $p \in [1, +\infty)$ as in formula 2.

Note this equation defines a family of aggregation functions depending on distance d and parameter p, which allows to consider the trade-offs between overall utility, fairness, and the influence of extreme positions. Table 2 provides guidelines for choosing p.

Utilitarian Aggregation ($p = 1$): With $p = 1$, equation 2 corresponds to minimising the *sum* of distances. This gives equal weight to every agent, delivering a median value system. Minority positions, however, exert negligible influence.

Use Case 3. A citywide participatory budget that has achieved high participation and is representative of the population. Utilitarian aggregation translates the majority's broadly shared priorities into a consensus value system without over-correcting for small extremist factions.

Table 2. Comparison of ethical paradigms with regards to Risk of Bias, Suitability with Low Dispersion Input (i.e. similar input value systems), Suitability with High Dispersion Input (i.e. cases with high polarisation), and Applicability.

	Utilitarian ($p = 1$)	**Rawlsian** ($p = \infty$)	**Intermediate** ($p > 1$)
Risk of Bias	Ignores minorities	Ignores majority	No risk
Suitability with LDI	Best. The result will be representative	Good as there are no major outliers.	Good as there are no major outliers.
Suitability with HDI	Bad. Minorities will not be represented	Best. The solutions is the fairest to outliers.	Good. Fair solution for everybody.
Applicability	Readily applicable	Readily applicable	Finding p is hard

Rawlsian Fairness ($p = \infty$): Setting $p = \infty$ minimises the *maximum* distance to any individual, thus ensuring maximum representativity and fairness. The approach may conflict with majority preferences when opinions are polarised.

Use Case 4. This aggregation method is suited for decision processes where it is important that minorities are given especial care. For example, funding accessibility upgrades (e.g. converting stairs to ramps) only benefits a minority of the population, hence decisions of this sort are bound to have low support. However, these changes greatly affect people with restricted mobility, if we want to be fair we have to give them heightened impact in the decision process. Rawlsian aggregation allows minority group's values to have as much impact in policy-making processes as possible.

Intermediate Paradigms ($p > 1$): Values of p between 1 and ∞ form a continuum that gradually amplifies outlier influence of minorities while preserving overall representativeness. Choosing p therefore becomes a policy lever for calibrated pluralism.

Use Case 5. As previously mentioned, high-income citizens are more likely to participate in participatory budgets than low-income citizens. Selecting an intermediate p can partially boost the under-represented low-income value systems, correcting turnout bias without completely eclipsing the majority.

6 General Vs Tailored Aggregation

Another important distinction among value-system aggregation methods is whether they are of *general* (i.e. usable in any domain) or *tailored* to one specific decision setting. The only published algorithm so far, the l_p-*regression* rule of Lera-Leri et al. [16], is a general purpose aggregation rule devised without a target application. This approach is ready to be applied straight away and in any scenario.

Table 3. Comparison of general and tailored aggregation approaches.

	General Approaches	**Tailored Approaches**
Availability	Readily available [16].	Not existent yet
Resources	Minimal economic and computational resources needed.	Investment needed. May not be computationally tractable.
Optimality	A "good enough" value system for most applications.	The resulting value system is optimal for the task at hand.

Use Case 6. A small municipality can estimate a city-wide value system with a general method, obtaining a good-enough input for participatory budget portals, without investing in upfront costs for a tailored aggregation.

Because value-system aggregation extends preference aggregation (Sect. 3), many contexts call for *tailored* aggregation methods which are engineered for a single policy domain and embed explicit moral or application-specific axioms. As indicated in Table 3, this precision comes at higher research, data, and computational cost, yet promises better results where generic rules fall short.

Example: Minimal Decision Divergence. Value system aggregation looks at finding a consensus value system but does not guarantee that the decisions made from that value system are also consensus decisions. To resolve this, we can tailor the aggregation process for this goal. We call **Minimal Decision Divergence (MDD)** the principle of aggregation methods whose aim is to ensure that the decisions made from the consensus aggregated value system are as similar as possible to the decisions each individual value system would lead to. A possible approach to achieve this is to define a distance-based aggregation function (see Equations 1, and 2) where the distance between two value systems is proportional to their decision divergence (i.e. how dissimilar the decisions produced by the two value systems are). In the case of participatory budgets, each citizen value system would lead to different proposals getting funded. Thus, our aim in aggregation is to find a consensus value system whose solution to the participatory budget allocation is as similar to the individual citizen solutions as possible.

Use Case 7. Tailored value system aggregation approaches are useful when the consequences of the decisions made from the aggregated value system are highly relevant, like in policymaking. However, tailored approaches need more economic and computational resources, so when these are not available, general approaches will represent sub-optimal but adequate solutions.

7 Alternatives to Aggregation

Beyond formal aggregation methods which employ mathematical calculations, collective value systems can emerge through *group decision-making* (GDM) processes, notably *multi-expert decision-making* (MEDM) [5,11]. MEDM has been

Table 4. Comparison of aggregation-based and deliberation-based methods.

	Aggregation-Based	**Deliberation-Based**
Imposition	Aggregation may impose an outcome.	Encourages voluntary compromises.
Reliability	Satisfies formal social choice properties	Prone to social biases (groupthink, polarization...)
Consistent outcomes	Yes. Same inputs yield same results.	No. Context and discussion affect results.
Time Consuming	Fast. One-shot decision-making.	Needs rounds of refinement.
Necessary input	Requires individual value systems obtained beforehand	There is no required input beforehand.
Participation	No recruiting necessary.	Recruiting citizens is necessary.

applied in AI governance [4], policy design [13], and forecasting [34], which highlights their real-world applicability.

Deliberation-based approaches seek consensus through iterative dialogue, as illustrated by assemblies [6,10,36]. They can surface hidden arguments and foster mutual understanding, but outcomes vary with group dynamics; biases such as *groupthink* [12] and *group polarisation* [35] may arise, and large-scale mobilisation is not expected. Many real systems mix the two logics. Sometimes even participatory budgets feature debates along with a voting phase [30]. The *Delphi method* [7] exemplifies a hybrid: anonymous, multi-round expert questionnaires iteratively refine judgments, mitigating social-bias pitfalls while ending in an aggregated result. Social-choice studies further show that even incomplete deliberation can yield *meta-agreements* on core concepts, easing subsequent aggregation [8,15,19,20,25]. Deliberation may thus shrink interpretation gaps highlighted in Sect. 4.

Use Case 8. Value inference (and therefore, value system aggregation) normally needs rich, labelled data [17]. A resource-constrained municipality could instead convene a citizen panel to deliberate and draft a shared value system, avoiding expensive surveys (Table 4).

8 Conclusions and Future Work

Understanding citizen values is of great utility for policymaking, however the process to obtain a model of citizen values, and in particular *value system aggregation* needs more research. This position paper has explored the possible lines of research to develop better value system aggregation methods with the aim of using them for value-aligned decision making. The sole published algorithm, l_p-*regression* [16], is a personal-judgement, general approach that spans ethical paradigms via a parameter. This means this approach would be useful to obtain a model of citizen values assuming we have tons of citizen data (not only their value preferences but how their understanding each value), we would have to know which ethical paradigm to use, and despite this apparent complexity, the aggregation is not tailored for any specific application. This setting is far from the usual, as governments usually have limited data on their citizens' value preferences, and may need approaches that are more tailored to sensible policy making applications. Future work will develop such specialised aggregators, beginning with the Minimal Decision Divergence criterion (Sect. 6).

Acknowledgments. Research funded by Ajuntament de Barcelona through Fundació Solidaritat UB, project code 25S03332-001. Marc Serramia is funded by project MMT24-IIIA-01. The funding for this contract comes from the European Union's Recovery and Resilience Facility-Next Generation, in the framework of the General Invitation of the Spanish Government's public business entity Red.es to participate in talent attraction and retention programmes within Investment 4 of Component 19 of the Recovery, Transformation and Resilience Plan.

References

1. Araque, O., Gatti, L., Kalimeri, K.: MoralStrength: exploiting a moral lexicon and embedding similarity for moral foundations prediction. Knowledge-Based Syst. **191**, 105184 (2020). https://doi.org/10.1016/j.knosys.2019.105184, https://www.sciencedirect.com/science/article/pii/S095070511930526X
2. Beauchamp, T.L., Childress, J.F.: Principles of Biomedical Ethics, 8th edn. Oxford University Press, New York (2019)
3. Brandt, F., Conitzer, V., Endriss, U., Lang, J., Procaccia, A.D.: Handbook of Computational Social Choice. Cambridge University Press, Cambridge, UK (2016)
4. Edwards, S.D.: AI in the noosphere: an alignment of scientific and wisdom traditions. AI Soc. **36**(1), 397–399 (2020). https://doi.org/10.1007/s00146-020-00999-9
5. Butler, C.L., Rothstein, A.: On Conflict and Consensus: A Handbook on Formal Consensus Decisionmaking. Food Not Bombs, Cambridge, MA (1991)
6. Convention Citoyenne pour le Climat: Final Report. https://www.conventioncitoyennepourleclimat.fr/en/ (2020). Accessed 10 Feb 2025
7. Dalkey, N., Helmer, O.: An experimental application of the DELPHI method to the use of experts. Manage. Sci. **9**(3), 458–467 (1963)
8. Dryzek, J.S., List, C.: Social choice theory and deliberative democracy: a reconciliation. British J. Polit. Sci. **33**(1), 1–28 (2003)
9. González-Pachón, J., Romero, C.: Bentham, Marx and Rawls ethical principles: in search for a compromise. Omega **62**, 47–51 (2016). https://doi.org/10.1016/j.omega.2015.08.008
10. Graeber, D.: The Democracy Project: A History, a Crisis, a Movement. Spiegel & Grau, New York, US (2013)
11. Huynh, V.N., Nakamori, Y.: Multi-expert decision-making with linguistic information: a probabilistic-based model. In: Proceedings of the Proceedings of the 38th Annual Hawaii International Conference on System Sciences (HICSS'05) - Track 3 - vol. 03, p. 91.3. HICSS '05, IEEE Computer Society, USA (2005). https://doi.org/10.1109/HICSS.2005.448

12. Janis, I.L.: Groupthink: Psychological Studies of Policy Decisions and Fiascoes, 2nd edn. Houghton Mifflin, Boston (1982)
13. Jones, M.: Integrating expert opinions in public policy development. Policy Stud. Rev. **32**(1), 89–110 (2015). https://doi.org/10.1111/psr.12075
14. Kendall, M.G.: A new measure of rank correlation. Biometrika **30**(1/2), 81–93 (1938). http://www.jstor.org/stable/2332226
15. Knight, J., Johnson, J.: Aggregation and deliberation: on the possibility of democratic legitimacy. Polit. Theory **22**(2), 277–296 (1994)
16. Lera-Leri, R., Bistaffa, F., Serramia, M., Lopez-Sanchez, M., Rodriguez-Aguilar, J.: Towards pluralistic value alignment: aggregating value systems through lp-regression. In: International Conference on Autonomous Agents and Multiagent Systems, pp. 780–788. AAMAS '22, IFAAMAS, Richland, SC (2022)
17. Liscio, E., et al.: Value inference in sociotechnical systems. In: International Conference on Autonomous Agents and Multiagent Systems, pp. 1774–1780. AAMAS '23, IFAAMAS, Richland, SC (2023)
18. Liscio, E., van der Meer, M., Siebert, L.C., Jonker, C.M., Murukannaiah, P.K.: What values should an agent align with? Autonomous agents and multi-agent systems **36**(1), 23 (2022). https://doi.org/10.1007/s10458-022-09550-0
19. List, C., Luskin, R.C., Fishkin, J.S., McLean, I.: Deliberation, single-peakedness, and the possibility of meaningful democracy: evidence from deliberative polls. J. Polit. **75**(1), 80–95 (2013)
20. Miller, D.: Deliberative democracy and social choice. Polit. Stud. **40**(S1), 54–67 (1992)
21. Noriega, P., Plaza, E.: On autonomy, governance, and values: an AGV approach to value engineering. In: Osman, N., Steels, L. (eds.) Value Eng. Artif. Intell., pp. 165–179. Springer Nature Switzerland, Cham (2024)
22. Paris, D.: Budget Participatif 2023 Resultats. https://www.paris.fr/pages/budget-participatif-2023-114-laureats-devoiles-25161 (2023). Accessed Feb 2024
23. Petitions: UK Government and Parliament. https://petition.parliament.uk/ (2015). Accessed Feb 2024
24. des pétitions, P.: Assemblée Nationale. https://petitions.assemblee-nationale.fr (2024). Accessed Feb 2024
25. Rafiee Rad, S., Roy, S.: Deliberation and single-peakedness: a computational study. J. Artif. Intell. Res. **70**, 1101–1130 (2021)
26. Ross, W.D.: The Right and the Good. Oxford University Press, Oxford (1930)
27. Saguin, K.: Why the poor do not benefit from community-driven development: lessons from participatory budgeting. World Develop. **112**, 220–232 (2018). https://doi.org/10.1016/j.worlddev.2018.08.009, https://www.sciencedirect.com/science/article/pii/S0305750X18303097
28. Scharfbillig, M., et al.: Values and identities - a policymaker's guide. Scientific analysis or review KJ-NA-30800-EN-N (online),KJ-NA-30800-EN-C (print),KJ-NB-30800-EN-Q, European Comission, Luxembourg (Luxembourg) (2021). https://doi.org/10.2760/349527 (online),10.2760/022780 (print),10.2760/059689
29. Schwartz, S.H.: An overview of the Schwartz theory of basic values. Online Read. Psychol. Cult. **2**(1), 0919–2307 (2012)

30. Serramia, M., et al.: Citizen support aggregation methods for participatory platforms. In: Sabater-Mir, J., Torra, V., Aguiló, I., Hidalgo, M.G. (eds.) Artificial Intelligence Research and Development - Proceedings of the 22nd International Conference of the Catalan Association for Artificial Intelligence, CCIA 2019, Mallorca, Spain, 23-25 October 2019. Frontiers in Artificial Intelligence and Applications, vol. 319, pp. 9–18. IOS Press, Amsterdam (2019). https://doi.org/10.3233/FAIA190102
31. Serramia, M., Lopez-Sanchez, M., Rodriguez-Aguilar, J.A., Moretti, S.: Value alignment in participatory budgeting. In: Proceedings of the 23rd International Conference on Autonomous Agents and Multiagent Systems, pp. 1692–1700. AAMAS '24, International Foundation for Autonomous Agents and Multiagent Systems, Richland, SC (2024)
32. Serramia, M., et al.: Encoding ethics to compute value-aligned norms. Minds Mach. **33**(4), 761–790 (2023). https://doi.org/10.1007/s11023-023-09649-7
33. Siebert, L.C., Liscio, E., Murukannaiah, P.K., Kaptein, L., Spruit, S., Van Den Hoven, J., Jonker, C.: Estimating value preferences in a hybrid participatory system. In: HHAI2022: Augmenting Human Intellect, pp. 114–127. IOS Press, Ansterdam, Netherlands (2022)
34. Smith, J.: Advanced Techniques in Forecasting. Academic Press, New York, NY (2010)
35. Sunstein, C.R.: Deliberation and polarization. Political. Philosophy **3**(1), 1–24 (2002). https://doi.org/10.1002/9780470693711.ch1
36. The Citizens' Assembly: The eighth amendment of the constitution. https://2016-2018.citizensassembly.ie/en/The-Eighth-Amendment-of-the-Constitution/ (2017). Accessed 10 feb 2025
37. Wilson, S.R., Shen, Y., Mihalcea, R.: Building and validating hierarchical lexicons with a case study on personal values. In: Staab, S., Koltsova, O., Ignatov, D.I. (eds.) Social Informatics, pp. 455–470. Springer International Publishing, Cham (2018)

Democracy as a Scaled Collective Intelligence Process: Points of Vulnerability and Augmentation

Marc-Antoine Parent(✉)

Conversence, Montréal, Canada
maparent@conversence.com
https://www.conversence.com

Abstract. The ideal democratic process aims to solve complex social decision problems, where diverse communities have potentially conflicting goals, through public deliberation, based on transparency, accountability, and trust. In practice, there are scaling limits to deliberative processes, both in terms of number of participants and cognitive complexity and democratic societies fall short of the ideal. Use of generative AI has been proposed to replace or augment the deliberative process. We argue that generative AI is an opaque process by nature, and hides issues with bias, power, accountability, and trust; and as such should not be directly involved in the decision-making process. We propose an alternate path, where decision-making is grounded in a fully transparent collective intelligence process, using a decision-oriented global structured knowledge base. Hybrid AI could help people approach and contribute to such a knowledge base, and watch over the coherence of expectations, actions and goals.

Keywords: Augmented collective intelligence · social learning · hybrid AI · deliberative process

1 Introduction: What Roles for AI in the Democratic Process?

With the popularization of generative AI, we have seen many proposals to use it to streamline many processes, including democratic governance or governance at large. Examples range from efforts to use generative AI to synthesize citizen consultations [10] or even facilitate them [32], rewrite legislation [33], engage with the public on behalf of politicians [16], etc. Schneier [51] gives many more examples.

There are also a proposals to replace the public service, and even democratic governance altogether with AI-driven processes. [20] This is based on a criticism of existing democratic institutions, which we want to analyze.

We propose to ask: what issues are these proposals trying to solve? Are their criteria of success aligned with those of democracy? What are those anyway?

J. Haqbeen et al. (Eds.): IJCAI 2025, LNAI 16400, pp. 28–47, 2026.
https://doi.org/10.1007/978-981-95-9667-6_3

What do we even mean by democracy? We will focus on two aspects of democracy, as a rational governance process and as a social negotiation, each with their distinct aims. We think identifying those will make it clearer where and how it is most and least appropriate to involve artificial intelligences in the process. In doing so, we will reuse the terminology for dimensions of democracy defined in [41].

2 Democracy as a Rational Governance Mechanism

Democracy is a specific form of social governance; we will start with a definition of what we mean by that term.

2.1 Governance Is a Decision-Making Process

Decision making can be modelled as follows: Given a known situation, an agent can take one of many actions. Each action has a range of expected consequences, according to a causal theory. Each consequence is valued, i.e. estimated to have a certain utility, according to goals expressed as a set criteria. The act of decision can be thought of as choosing an action that maximizes aggregate utility according to those expectations and criteria.

In a collective setting (whether organization or political), every individual bases decisions on an heuristics, which is based on a simplified causal theory, but also on a collective agreement about the most appropriate actions to take in a given situation. These agreements can be implicit (cultural norms, [46]) or explicit (rule of law).

2.2 Governance Involves Continuous Learning

Decisions do not always yield the hoped-for outcome, and every decision outcome is an opportunity to correct one's action. In some cases, the outcome is not deeply surprising, and it is possible to correct course directly, without revising one's causal theory, or with minor tunings of likelihood estimates (L1); in other cases, the change requires revising the underlying abstract causal schema (L2), or even re-evaluating the goals (L3); in the more radical cases, the process through which we imagine and evaluate competing causal theories must itself be re-evaluated (L4). These layers of learning have been called single, double and triple-loop learning respectively, by diverse researchers, though the definitions sometimes overlap. (My L4 is usually included in the third loop.) [2,8,24,55]

At any scale, the individual or collective's success depends on the accuracy of their heuristics. As we accumulate experience in a complex world, we realize simplified heuristics cannot at the same time reflect that complexity accurately, and fit within the bounds of any individual's cognitive capacity. This means both that it requires greater cognitive capacity to maintain the heuristic's factual accuracy, and also that individual decisions are constrained by the complexity of the heuristics.

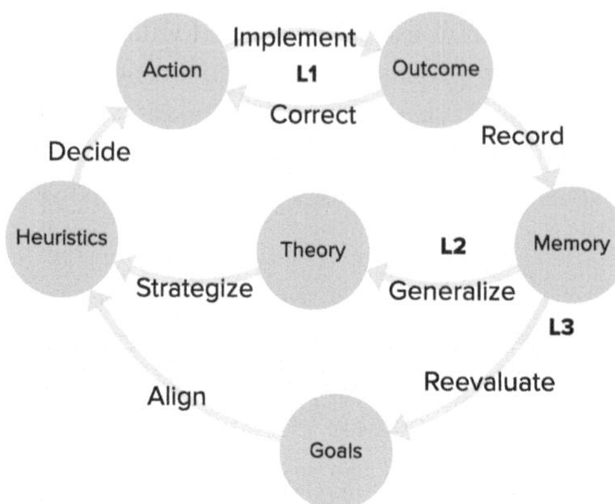

Fig. 1. Decisions and learning loops

Criterion 1 (Accuracy). Actions should be guided by heuristics that reflect a causal theory that is accurate enough.

Criterion 2 (Legibility). The decision heuristics should be simple enough to be understandable by members of the collective.

Criterion 3 (Cognitive Capacity). Cognitive capacity should be adequate to generalize a theory from the learned experience, and distill it into a heuristic aligned with the goals.

Criterion 4 (Learning). Experiences should be captured, and be available in a shared memory. There should be a continuous effort to maintain that memory, and learn from it.

Trade-off 1. Thus, we can identify a first trade-off, between Accuracy and Cognitive Capacity.

2.3 Collective Intelligence

Deciding entities have to make decisions from partial knowledge of the situation, using an incomplete causal theory[1] built from limited experience, using limited rationality, subject to cognitive biases [34]. Fortunately, these limitations can be alleviated by drawing on collective intelligence.

Many teams and small tribes take decisions after deliberation. It has been shown that deliberation improves the Accuracy of decisions, under certain conditions. Those conditions include a shared goal and sufficient diversity to avoid groupthink. It has even been hypothesized that the evolution of human cognition was mostly driven by its usage in a social context, as confirmation bias can be

[1] Assuming the situation's causal regime even allows predictions, as opposed to chaos or emergent dynamics, [52].

a heuristic leading to an efficient division of cognitive labour, and the resulting inaccuracy gets corrected by iterations in a social context [39].

A more abstract argument can be made in favour of deliberative cognition: As originally stated by Ashby [3], any entity (individual or collective) that wants to adapt to the world should have adequate inner complexity to have the capacity to detect, understand (a causal theory), and react to the states of the world that affect it. Again a group with sufficiently diverse expertise and points of views is more likely to have the requisite variety. So there is a diversity angle to Cognitive Capacity.

Criterion 5 (Diversity). Accuracy relies on an adequate diversity of expertise and points of view in the conversation

On the other hand, there is a communication overhead to deliberation, which scales quadratically with group size, and even a diverse group can succumb to groupthink. This is why, beyond a certain scale, the various functions of the decision and learning process are handed to separate institutions, as discussed in Sect. 3.1.

Criterion 6 (Overhead). Decision processes should not become bogged down in coordination and communication overhead.

3 Democracy as a Socio-Political Process

Democracy is also a socio-political process, where diverse publics, with sometimes conflicting interests, negotiate a shared way of life [22,40]. A large part of the democratic process in particular is determination of a set of coherent social goals from the aggregated goals of all sub-communities, or all citizens. It is also possible that the goals of sub-communities are too profoundly different for any set of common goals to satisfy any of them, which may lead to social fragmentation[2].

Criterion 7 (Cohesion). The goals of sub-communities in the collective remain compatible enough that the sub-communities engage in the higher-level goal of trying to align them, rather than splitting the community.

Given enough cohesion, the next step in the democratic process is choosing a strategy for collective actions, so they align with collective goals. Again, shared heuristics and social norms allow coordinated actions without Overhead of coordination [50]. This is why, in a social context, people give value to following norms, rather than optimization for individualistic best outcome [46].

Criterion 8 (Alignment). Heuristics and subsequent decisions should be aligned with stated collective goals.

[2] Often in a feedback loop of antagonism, first described by Bateson in [7] as schismogenesis.

According to Rawls [48], it is possible for subgroups in a pluralistic society to agree on actions without agreeing on underlying goals, leading to what Rawls describes as a *modus vivendi.* From there, trust can build in time, and subgroups can identify local areas of agreement on goals from which to build further trust, even though global agreement remains provisionally out of reach. A society can function using this *overlapping consensus.* As such, both coherence and alignment are often a continuous work in process.

But the important point here is that the process itself matters: citizens and communities learn to trust the shared rules and social conventions insofar as they feel they are actively involved in the processes that shape the social consensus and its implementation.

Criterion 9 (Participation). The public can and does get involved in the various steps of the decision and learning loop[3].

Of course, this involvement only makes sense if the process implementation actually follows the heuristics (rules or norms) that have been decided through goal alignment, strategy, goal aggregation and knowledge generalization. In the words of Elliot Higgins of Bell¿ngcat [30], democracy needs:

Criterion 10 (Verification). Processes for truth-checking, and for checking that actions follow the stated rules.

Criterion 11 (Deliberation). Ideas are discussed in public forums

Criterion 12 (Accountability). A process to respond to decisions that fail (whether with sanctions or revised learning)

Processes and learning It can be argued that the type of social, collective learning involved here is of a fundamentally different type than the factual learning involved in updating a causal theory, or discovering implementation strategies. This social learning can be situated in what Weber called the lifeworld (*lebenswelt*) [58], the fabric of socialization, social integration, and reproduction of culture and society. This reproduction is both transmission of social learning and a continuous self-redefinition, what Castoriadis called autonomy [12], or Varela called autopoïesis [38]. Weber, and later Parsons and Habermas, opposed the lifeworld to what they called the system, social subsystems dedicated to short-term utilitarian optimization. They both argue that the system has its place, but should not "colonize" the transmission processes of the lifeworld [28,29].

[3] See conditions and criteria for democratic processes in [41], which defines: Representation, Informedness, Accuracy, Deliberation, Substantiveness (2), Robustness, Legibility, Commitment, Integration, Ability to bind, Awareness, Participation, 12, and Buy-in.

3.1 Institutions

The institution of representative democracy is a specific institution that attempts to avoid oligarchy through periodic replacement of the deciding bodies, themselves arranged in a balance of power. This replacement function is only one accountability process among many steps in the social learning loop, and there are complementary institutions that ensure other steps. Much is made of the separation of powers into legislative, executive and judicial branches; those would map to the alignment, implementation, and correction steps in the decision diagram. But social decision and learning involves many sectors of society, and those heuristics which are encoded as law are but a fraction of social decisions. To name a few:

- Bureaucracy: involved in the implementation phase of decisions, but also collecting memory (L1)
- Academia: involved in building the causal theory from accumulated experience (L2)
- Journalism: directs public attention towards discrepancies between goals and outcomes, effectively triage-ing the correction function (L1-4)
- Auditors: Identifying issues that need to be corrected (L1)
- Civil society: Either advocating for the correction of issues or implementing them (L1, L3)
- Citizen assemblies: Tasked with checking the alignment with the heuristics with sufficient requisite diversity (L3)
- Artists: Reshaping the narratives around certain goals, through which cultural norms adapt (L3)

The bureaucracy is an important case in point. Ostensibly, is there to carry out decisions of a deciding body. But more importantly, it connects a smaller deciding body, such as those of representative democracy or citizen assemblies, with a body of domain experts, either from the scholarly community or trained by them, who will advise the deciding bodies when relevant (1). As such, it can augment the cognitive capacity of the deciding body to match the complexity of the issues being considered (3). It also acts as a specific shared memory for decisions and goals, allowing memorization and Verification, and at its best can even ensure that different aspects of a complex and extensive strategy do not work at cross-purpose.

Criterion 13 (Coherence). Social actions should not be at cross-purpose. Ultimately, expected consequences should be considered based on global combination of actions, not on individual actions.

Dividing the work in this way allows for specialized teams to take on specific challenges, but the complexity of coordination is pushed to the inter-group level. A particular set of institutions, and more important how they interact, embodies the political infrastructure of a given society or organization, and rethinking this configuration of institutions belongs in the fourth layer of the learning loop.

Trade-off 2. But here lurks another trade-off: though there is a benefit in coherent action (13), it may come at the expense of adapting to the Diversity of specific situations. Bureaucracy is far removed from the local reality of communities and their specific lifeworlds.

3.2 Agonistics

When defining common goals from the goals of agonistic sub-communities, there are many different aggregation strategies, with different trade-offs, and some may lead to the goals of a majority, or an oligarchic minority, dominating the decision process.

Criterion 14 (Fairness). Social processes, in particular the process used to determine collective goals, should not systematically ignore the goals of a sub-community.

We will not recapitulate political theory here, but would like to point out that an important part of the conflict plays out at two levels: trying to influence public opinion (whether through information or disinformation campaigns), and trying to influence the deciders, which represent a smaller attack surface[4].

Representative democracy creates its own elites: The complexity of the state apparatus makes it more likely to be captured by an expert class of its own, which may itself suborn the process to its own interests. Of course, the complexity of the system of institutions partly reflects the complexity of the world and society; and it has been argued (as far back as Plato) that allowing the broader public to have a say in important decisions is a guarantee for uninformed decisions.

But a specialized political class has its own downsides. For example, it is advantageous for candidate representatives to use vague promises as a way to garner support from people with ultimately divergent interests, at the expanse of Legibility and Accountability. The end result is that citizens lose trust in the processes, and rightly so: in a recent study, it was shown that political decisions in the USA were systematically biased in favour of elite interests against citizen preferences [26]. The complexity of the state also becomes a way to avoid Verification.

3.3 Cognitive Complexity Revisited

On the other hand, experiments with direct democracy have lead to sets of law that are faulted for Accuracy, Coherence, or both. Successful experiments with collective intelligence with a fair, representative sample of the broader public, such as citizen assemblies [18] and deliberative polling [23], have relied on an extensive (6) deliberative process, where experts are readily available to explain the issue clearly.

---

[4] Corruption of public officials is an ancient problem, which is why Athenian democracy resorted to sortition [49]. Corruption is more common in more unequal societies.

Trade-off 3. And we see another key, more complex trade-off: Accuracy, especially when dealing with social Diversity requires a deliberative process (11); but that process has a cost both in communication Overhead and in Legibility of complex issues.

For each step in our model 1 of decision and learning, we should identify institutions in charge of that step, and how they handle those tradeoffs identified. To caricature extreme models, libertarians favour adaptation to diversity at the expense of coherence (and cohesion); oligarchs sacrifice accuracy (and deliberation) to coherence; technocratic bureaucracy represent a compromise of coherence and accuracy that sacrifices legibility. Can we improve on the institutions of democracy without creating a prohibitive overhead? In particular, how to make the social decisions and learning, in all their complexity, subject to verification, deliberation and accountability?

3.4 Social Media Agora

As a counterpoint, let us look at how social media has claimed the role of an agora, where everybody can weigh in on public issues, including governance. This is clearly a more inclusive and diverse Deliberation than criticism through professionalized classes (such as journalists or civil society activists).

*Objection (*Cohesion*).* However, a downside of social media, with its emphasis on engagement, is that it naturally favours strong emotional reactions, such as anger and fear. This can lead to rising hostility between factions, up to the point where they interact from a basic stance of distrust. This distrust is compounded in that, pursuing engagement, social media has an incentive to feed the emotions with "more of the same", leading different factions to live in an information bubble.

*Objection (*Accuracy*).* This could be mitigated with fact-checking against a shared reality, but accuracy is also sacrificed to engagement.

*Objection (*Legibility*).* Another issue with social media is that each contribution stands on its own, and is not necessarily connected to similar interventions except through replying. It is very hard to have an intelligible map of how many distinct ideas are being expressed, and who stands behind each one.

*Objection (*Learning*).* Beyond the duplication issue, the ephemeral stream conversation structure of social media makes it harder than necessary to cross-reference new interventions against past interventions, which prevents the accumulation of a stock of learning.

4 Issues with Generative AI as a Core Governance Mechanism

Given these existing mechanisms and criteria, let us ask again what roles should automated processes play? We would like to specifically make arguments against involving them in the decision making itself.

4.1 Inherent Biases

The basic argument for using generative AI is that it provides deciders convenient access to a broad synthesis of human knowledge. This itself is a form of synthesis of Diversity. A more speculative argument is made that generative AI can or will someday provide original answers to difficult problems, but let us first focus on the current state of the technology.

*Objection (*Accuracy*).* At some basic level, generative AI acts as a (lossy) compression of its training set. As such, it has been shown to blindly reproduce existing biases in its training set [59]. The only sure way to prevent that would be to fact-check the training set, but that is not economically realistic given the size of the training set needed to train a modern generative AI. So instead of fact-checking, generative AI relies on the internal consistency of the training set as an imperfect proxy for accuracy.

*Objection (*Verification*).* Of course, another reason fact-checking is not done is that the training set is expected to be an industrial secret, to create a moat in the AI company's business model. The implication is that the training set cannot in general be verified.

Introspection. There is a huge research effort ongoing to provide explainable AI, so that AI suggestions can be verified even if the process itself is a black box. Some of this effort is looking at the internal weights, but this type of explanation is hard to understand (2) and does not help to check the provenance of the AI's statement, or to engage in Deliberation around it.

Most people rely on the imperfect proxy of asking the generative AI why it choose an answer. When prompted to do so, the generative AI will indeed provide the most likely explanation that someone would give when asked such a question. This is pure confabulation, and has nothing to do with the AI's inner mechanism, which is opaque to its training-set regurgitation mechanism. Furthermore, it is based on human *post hoc* justification of their own positions, which is also generally understood to be quite unaware of the factors actually involved in the inner decision mechanism. Humans are not generally good at introspection either.

In a social reasoning process, this flaw is mitigated by the process of conversation, where reasons can be subject to discussion, under the assumption of equality 14.

Human Reception. This assumption obviously does not hold when humans converse with AI; their considerable recall and polished language make most people take answers from generative AI as more authoritative than they are.

Generative AIs are also very unreliable conversation partners for many reasons; much has been made of so-called hallucinations, but it's only lately that people are more overtly critical of the impact on our inherent confirmation bias of the sycophancy that AI has been programmed to display, probably to be more agreeable to customers [25]. The agreeableness is also problematic in its own right; there have been studies of cases of emotional dependency on AIs as emotional support [61], but there have also been concerns whether heavy AI users will lose the skills to handle a clash of views in a productive way.

Biases as an Expression of Power

Objection (Accuracy, Alignment). In the most extreme cases, the opacity of the process enables covert manipulation by people who choose to introduce bias, either in the form of unfounded claims, such as Grok's recent assertion of white genocide [35], or the poisoning of training set by russian propaganda [17].

Given those issues, one can question the enthusiasm to push generative AI into the decision process.

One obvious reason is financial: The sellers of generative AI solutions have an incentive to sell those solutions at all layers, and the decision layer of decision bodies, whether at the social or corporate level, is an extremely lucrative one. This opportunity for AI companies comes to the detriment of knowledge workers whose work was either part of the knowledge commons or private, and was enclosed by inclusion in training sets.

Objection (Fairness). Meanwhile, small circles of deciders have a financial incentive not to employ those same knowledge workers, and to replace them with automated processes. But there is also an ideological battleground, where deciders can resent the interventions of experts, especially when these experts' evidence questions the validity of decisions that were taken against the public interest, following corruption or capture. Replacing experts with a mechanism makes it much more convenient to camouflage the goals of any decision. More generally, the more decision is automated, the less other people are involved in the decision.

This is especially obvious in the workplace: generative AI is often imposed on workers, often with the explicit aim of replacing them. There are no democratic principles of equality in work communities, and even in the political community, there are actors whose explicit plan is to replace processes in human institutions, which they deem fallible, by even more fallible automated decision processes [15].

4.2 Accountability Sink

Objection (Accountability). There is another incentive: Letting opaque algorithms take decisions is a way to obscure the chain of decision, and makes it extremely difficult to require any accountability for bad decisions. Thus deciders become both able to introduce bias opaquely and become unaccountable for failure.

The usual answer of AI proponents to accuracy issues (besides claiming it's going to get better *real soon now*) is proposing that someone should vet the answers of the AI, the so-called human in the loop. However, verification of information does not require less time or cognitive effort than research. Meanwhile, the speed of generation imposes a rhythm to information flow that makes thorough verification impractical. Of course, the overall effect is a decrease of fact-checking and accuracy, and even of the capacity to do so [37]. Most important, the human in the loop will be scapegoated for the unavoidable mistakes, and rarely the person who put the system in place. This is another way in which opaque algorithms act as an accountability sink [21].

4.3 Short-Circuiting Social Learning

Finally, there is broad concern about the impact of generative AI on the capacity to learn. Some aspects are rather obvious, such as the providing a bread opportunity for cheating, and fostering intellectual laziness.

*Objection (*Learning*).* Another well known issue is that generative AIs, though they cannot (yet?) replace experts, can and do replace novices in many professions. How will the next generation learn to become experts if they do not have access to the learning and mentorship opportunities of a novice position?

But there is a more subtle issue: Generative AI is trained on past information. It can be retrained with new information, but does not behave well if the new information includes AI output. Since we do not have provenance information in our training sets, we cannot practically exclude AI output, and training AI with updated data is more and more difficult. Even if that were the case, AI is, through training, essentially backwards-looking, offering new combinations of past statements, but there is a level of innovation that may be inherently beyond it. There is no doubt it can handle single-loop corrections, and probably some simple double-loop learning, but there is a possibility that triple-loop learning is fundamentally beyond its reach, at least on its own.

By interacalating itself in social processes, a uniquely insidious colonization of the lifeworld, generative AI short-circuits the processes of cultural transmission by which social learning may otherwise occur.

4.4 Whose Conversation?

*Objection (*Participation*).* For trust, the process matters as much as its result, and this would be true even if the automated (human-less) process were to yield perfect, ideal consensus. Without the process of deliberation and value alignment itself, there cannot arise a feeling of being part of a community, and the political unit is reduced to its rawest power dimension: you are a citizen because the laws of the nation declare you are, however you feel about it.

Again, there is nothing inherently wrong with including generative AI in a public deliberation process, as long as participants understand the strengths and limitations of generative AI. The issue is when the AI is either taking decisions, or in an opaque dialogue with a decision body. It is both vindicating and troubling that one of the most promising avenues of research in AI is having multiple AI agents in a conversation together; again, the issue is that they're having this deliberation among themselves, without including us.

5 Augmented Collective Intelligence

We propose a programme to research and realize augmented collective intelligence at scale. It takes as fundamental the value of transparent deliberation, and proposes that all decisions should be grounded in a comprehensive deliberative map.

5.1 Historical Precedent: Dialogue Mapping

In its original form, dialogue mapping has been shown to work best for groups of medium size, who discuss in an assembly, while a cartographer constructs a map of the discussion i real time. The map represents key issues, proposals and arguments. Unlike a pure debate map, new questions can arise at any point. It has been found that the map, as a liminal object, can defuse tensions, as people address the point rather than the person who first enounced it. Dialogue mapping has been found to help very diverse communities, with diverging goals, reach a mutual understanding [19]. Interestingly, this does not carry over if participants were asked to do their own mapping asynchronously [11]. This was partly due to contributions that were not following the mapping conventions, but another issue was some people clogging up the map with detailed description of side issues, until the global map was barely legible.

5.2 Towards a Global Map for Collective Intelligence

Why a Map? We strongly believe that natural language is ill-suited as a working memory for large-scale collective intelligence. Each idea can have countless different expressions. On the one hand, there is clear pedagogical value to what Mike Caulfield calls choral explanations, [13], allowing people with diverse backgrounds to understand an idea in a form appropriate to their expertise. Gathering those multiple formulations as a single point on the map reduces the communication Overhead, and the overwhelm and cognitive complexity.

Also, a map can directly display the extent of the alternative space in the neighbourhood of a given idea, helping people become aware of how much they don't know yet. We believe that this awareness might encourage at least some people to at least consider other perspectives.

Progressive Formalization. As ideas on the map have multiple expressions, understandable by a diversity of people, we propose this diversity includes structural descriptions of ideas, using formal language and symbolic data structures. Formal languages have the benefit of reducing ambiguity, and hence Accuracy. Formalized ideas can be compared using various formal analysis techniques, allowing to de-duplicate equivalent ideas, identify inconsistencies (helping Coherence), etc. However, formal languages are usually designed by domain experts, and hard to approach by outsiders.

Trade-off 4. Thus, there is normally a trade-off between the precise vocabulary needed for Accuracy, and including (9) a broader (14) public in the Deliberation. This is related to the trade-off 1 with cognitive complexity.

This non-specialist public might approach the map through the choral explanations in natural language, but a hybrid (symbolic-generative) AI can also play a helpful role, translating the more symbolic knowledge in vernacular terms. To enable them to participate actively in the conversation (14), we must also accept informal, unstructured contributions. But then, we can progressively help them to clarify their contribution: we can identify ambiguities and ask clarifying questions; we can suggest multiple interpretations, and ask contributors to commit to (at least) one of them; we can compare it to already-formalized ideas, and ask to focus on the distintive elements; we can propose breaking it down into component concepts. Eventually, the contribution will be clear enough to be formalized. This whole process can be crowdsourced with peers, or with the mentorship of hybrid AI.

Indicators. The map will serve the function of global memory insofar as it is exhaustive. An exhaustive global map will be, by essence, too large to be legible. People will interact with the global memory through either curated or computed maps. Maps curated by humans, making editorial choices, are more likely to have high Legibility, and be the most useful for approaching the information space. Of course, they will reflect the biases of their authors. As the curated map is embedded in a global information map, the system can provide indicators that express the scope of what's outside the map. Useful partial maps can also be computed by the system, based on traversing relations and using indicators as heuristics to prune elements beyond a certain number.

This is one of the most delicate aspects of the system: heuristics for indicators can re-introduce hidden bias. First, the algorithms for indicators should themselves be transparent, and subject to public Deliberation. More controversially, the system should allow to incorporate a Diversity of aggregation and ranking indicators, much like Bluesky's open marketplace of algorithms [27]. However, in the name of Verification, closed-sourced algorithms should be marked as such. The system should make it convenient to re-compute any view incorporting unverified indicators in a way that compares them to a set of publically vetted indicators. On the other hand, we do not believe in excluding them outright; the plurality of approaches may itself contribute to make it more difficult to game the system.

What indicators are we considering as central?

Abstraction and Distinctions. A fundamental issue with a global map is to present a cluster of a great number of related ideas in the form of a unifying abstraction at the right level. Though we can use automated semantic clustering to identify tentative clusters, we propose to use techniques from formal concept analysis [60] to interpret them as a lattice of abstractions and distinctions, progressively lending structure to the massive underlying knowledge base. We can then use indicators of usage to make informed guesses about the appropriate level of abstraction, or the most salient distinctions, for a given participant. In case of error, the participant should be able to navigate the structure.

Coherence Indicators. A deliberation tool should not be an arbiter of truth, and needs to record a plurality of viewpoints. Yet, especially in this era of weaponized disinformation and cognitive denial of service attacks with a flood of nonsensical information, we cannot totally eschew the responsibility to rate information. We believe that fighting disinformation requires incorporating it, and to identify the presence of supporting or contradicting evidence. As such, the platform should focus on Coherence issues, between decisions, misalignments with goals, or conflicting goals. (Though sometimes those represent a legitimate balance.) Again, some of this will be crowdsourced, but hybrid AI could be invaluable in the automated detection of suspected inconsistencies and maybe broader coherence issues in the decision base. Such potential issues would then be subject to further human deliberation, or the structured information could also be checked by classical, verifiable inference engines.

Here, we believe there is much space for research in identifying algorithms that help the process of deliberation. Some indicators may focus on content, others on the communication structure. For example, the global brain [57] measures how much each individual contribution pushes participants towards the position of maximally involved (and presumably informed) participants. We believe, but would like to verify, that debates could be improved by directing participant's attention to higher-level learning loop elements, such as epistemic criteria: what would lead them to believe a position against the other? One part of the proposal is that we should share an experimental workbench to study such issues.

Moderation. In any system that accepts public contributions, we have to tackle the issue of moderation. Beyond the obvious (hate speech), we have to deal with arguments that oppose the value of inclusive deliberation as a basis for decision making. Despite the paradox of tolerance [47], we are committed to mapping such positions, precisely so they can be refuted. However, such positions are contrary to the goals of the platform, and will be tagged as such, and the original unstructured contribution containing may still be filtered out.

Reputation. This is another sensitive design area. We acknowledge the value of debating at the level of ideas, not people. Abstracted, structured ideas can be partially detached from their authors. There is a lot of research in the positive value of avatars in certain epistemic settings. Yet, there is also a strong value in tracing provenance of ideas, if only to distinguish contributions of humans, artificial or collective actors. Also, though *ad hominem* is in principle a fallacy, a lot of legitimate political debate concerns statements by individuals, their interpretation and consequence, and anonymity only goes so far. More importantly, using provenance, we can measure the track record of contributors [54] and institutions. This can be incorporated as a key proxy indicator to rank arguments.

Trade-off 5. There is a trade-off between allowing a track report of reliable information to play a role in ranking contributions, and not letting powerful or famous people dominate the discussion.

Federation. In our experience, people rarely converge on a single technical infrastructure. Indeed, just as expert communities need jargon for efficient communication, they need diverse domain-specific tools to manipulate the concepts of their discipline. Consequently, we do not propose a single tool, but a commitment to an ecosystem of tools that share an interoperable data format. This format should allow for federated cross-references between multiple thinking repositories, or (in the terms of Jack Park) knowing hubs, and for third parties to compute aggregated indicators across the federation.

What would such a data format look like? We have contributed to an early federation protocol for collective intelligence [43], which was based on the basic categories used in dialogue mapping: a few concepts (questions, proposals and arguments) and relations (answers, pro, con, questions.) This is a simple and proven core, but we suspect that structured conversation will benefit from a richer vocabulary. In particular, since we are dealing with decisions, the notion of expected outcome, and valuation along criteria, needs to be part of that vocabulary.

Experts have identified a on the order of a hundred argumentation schemes [56], and on the order of a thousand linguistic frames describing basic situations [5]. Which of those are necessary? We do not believe that the perfect vocabulary exists to be identified, but that we should allow for a language to evolve through Learning, in the form of accretion around a base core, guided by usage statistics. However, to avoid this to become a babel, we have proposed to use nested frames [42]. Frame nesting is formally equivalent to a recursive hypergraph, and allows statements about statements. New frame proposals should strive to build upon simpler frames through composition, and/or to provide a translation layer to alternate proposals. The translation layer should be determinstic and work at the level of structured data, though the result may take the form of a less formal linking frame.

6 Parallel Work and Open Issues

This is a research program, and we do not have all the answers. Yet we are building on established research, and we find many researchers are building parts of what we're proposing, besides the components we are ourselves experimenting with.

First, there is a lot of activity around structured conversation [36]. We have previously been involved in one such project, where among other things we experimented with visualization and deliberation analytics [44]. We are currently involved with discourse graphs, which develops structured conversations for research teams [14].

Experiments also show that generative AI can be used to automate the generation of conversation maps [10]. Such generated maps can be shown improve group discussions [1,32]. Conversational agents have also been shown to be skilled at moderation [4], and have been shown to help polarized groups reach a better mutual understanding [53]. In the latter case, the effect could be explained in part to the persisting attribution of neutrality to automated processes by the participants, but either way, we believe strongly in the possibility of harnessing AI's access to a considerable corpus to identify bridges between epistemic islands, in community with people willing to do the exercise. We also hope that demonstrating this possibility will get people to reconsider the value of the deliberative process to create more Coherence in society.

The idea of a global map of knowledge is ancient, and the origins of the internet can be traced to this dream, from Vannevar Bush's memex, to Ted Nelson's Xanadu, to Tim Berner Lee's web [6]. Trying to build a global map specific to deliberation and decision making also has precedents, such as DebateWise, and recently the Canonical Debate Map white paper of Timothy High [31]. We have shared ideas on knowledge federation with Jack Park of TopicQuests, and previously we had worked on a collective intelligence data interoperability format [43] for the Catalyst project.

This history is one of partial successes and failures. The internet has provided a shared addressing space for documents, and WikiPedia has provided a reference point for ideas.

Yet, at the rational level, attempts at deeper knowledge unification have remained marginal. What is our strategy to avoid this fate? First, we are not trying to build a unifying ontology, but embrace ontological pluralism. We believe that, thanks to the role of hybrid AI as a translator, there is a unique opportunity to resolve the tradeoff 4 between crowdsourcing and formalization.

At the social levol, many important conversations happen within silos, whether for convenience, comfort or a (partly illusory) feeling of privacy. We believe one deep underlying issue is that there are strong social disincentives to make the decision processes public. Accountability can create an enormous pressure to avoid even the appearance of considering impopular options; whereas in reality it would be better to consider and reject them for explicit reasons. But even without those pressures, it can be useful to let unfinished ideas compost in small trusted groups, to avoid premature exposure or even premature formal explicitation. (Nora Bateson calls this process aphanipoiesis [9].) This is another reason to allow for federated, community-based knowledge hubs; some ideas can be made public when ready. But there also needs to be a higher social tolerance for nuance and tentative exploration and experiments. Again, we hope that laying out the process (even with delay) will make this more acceptable, and facilitate higher levels of social learning.

We also believe firmly in the importance of making structured deliberation more accessible to the general public, both through using generative AI as a translator/mentor, and through pedagogical activities. In particular, we are developing a coopetitive game with Jack Park [45], where teams learn to contribute to a structured conversation.

Beyond this project and research agenda, we hope that this paper sparks a discussion of the precise risks and benefits that AI pose at various points in the decision model.

Acknowledgments. Many of these ideas were developed with Jack Park, of TopicQuests. I am also grateful to Sonny Bhatia of West Point, and Louise Vandelac of UQAM, for helpful comments.

Ethical Statement. There are no ethical issues in our research at this stage.

References

1. Anastasiou, L., Liddo, A.D.: Bcause: Human-ai collaboration to improve hybrid mapping and ideation in argumentation-grounded deliberation (2025). https://arxiv.org/abs/2505.03584
2. Argyris, C., Schön, D.A.: Theory in Practice: Increasing Professional Effectiveness. Jossey-Bass, San Francisco (1974)
3. Ashby, W.R.: Requisite variety and its implications for the control of complex systems. Cybernetica **1**(2) (1958)
4. Babatunde, I.D., Nnanna, O.M., Klein, M.: Moderating large scale online deliberative processes with large language models (llms): enhancing collective decision-making. In: Proceedings of the 40th ACM/SIGAPP Symposium on Applied Computing. p. 996–1003. SAC '25, Association for Computing Machinery, New York, NY, USA (2025). https://doi.org/10.1145/3672608.3707925
5. Baker, C.: FrameNet, present and future. In: Webster, J., Ide, N., Fang, A.C. (eds.) The First International Conference on Global Interoperability for Language Resources. City University, City University, Hong Kong (2008)
6. Balasubramanian, V.: State of the art review on hypermedia issues and applications (1993)
7. Bateson, G.: Naven: A Survey of the Problems Suggested by a Composite Picture of the Culture of a New Guinea Tribe Drawn from Three Points of View. Cambridge University Press, Cambridge (1936)
8. Bateson, G.: Steps to an Ecology of Mind: Collected Essays in Anthropology, Psychiatry, Evolution and Epistemology, chap. Social Planning and the Concept of Deutero-Learning. Paladin, Granada, London (1942)
9. Bateson, N.: Aphanipoiesis. https://norabateson.medium.com/aphanipoiesis-96d8aed927bc
10. Bhatia, A., Sukthankar, G.: Using LLMs to structure and visualize policy discourse. In: Yin, W., et al. (eds.) Artificial Intelligence for Research and Democracy, pp. 69–76. Springer Nature Singapore, Singapore (2025)
11. Buckingham Shum, S.J., Selvin, A.M., Sierhuis, M., Conklin, J., Haley, C.B., Nuseibeh, B.: Rationale Management in Software Engineering, chap. Hypermedia Support for Argumentation-Based Rationale: 15 Years on from gIBIS and QOC, pp. 111–132. Computer Science Editorial, Springer-Verlag (2006), http://kmi.open.ac.uk/publications/index.cfm?trnumber=kmi-05-18
12. Castoriadis, C.: L'institution imaginaire de la société. Seuil, Paris (1975)

13. Caulfield, M.: Choral explanations. https://hapgood.us/2016/05/13/choral-explanations/ (2016)
14. Chan, J., Akamatsu, M., Vargas, D., Kawerau, L., Gartner, M.: Steps towards an infrastructure for scholarly synthesis. https://arxiv.org/abs/2407.20666 (2024)
15. Chayka, K.: Elon musk's a.i.-fuelled war on human agency. The New Yorker (2025). https://www.newyorker.com/culture/infinite-scroll/elon-musks-ai-fuelled-war-on-human-agency
16. Christopher, N., Bansal, V.: Indian voters are being bombarded with millions of deepfakes. political candidates approve (2024). https://www.wired.com/story/indian-elections-ai-deepfakes/
17. Châtelet, V.: Exposing pravda: How pro-kremlin forces are poisoning ai models and rewriting wikipedia (2025). https://www.atlanticcouncil.org/blogs/new-atlanticist/exposing-pravda-how-pro-kremlin-forces-are-poisoning-ai-models-and-rewriting-wikipedia/
18. Collective: European citizens' assembly: a new model for decision making. Technical report, Center for Blue Democracy (2022). https://citizensassemblies.org/wp-content/uploads/2022/05/European-Citizens-Assembly.pdf
19. Conklin, J.: Dialogue Mapping: Building Shared Understanding of Wicked Problems. John Wiley & Sons (2006)
20. Danaher, J.: The threat of algocracy: reality, resistance and accommodation. Philosop. Technol. **29**(3), 245–268 (2016). https://doi.org/10.1007/s13347-015-0211-1
21. Doctorow, C.: Ai's "human in the loop" isn't (2024). https://pluralistic.net/2024/10/30/a-neck-in-a-noose/
22. Farrell, H., Han, H.: Ai and democratic publics. Technical report, 25-17 Knight First Amend. Inst. (2025). https://knightcolumbia.org/content/ai-and-democratic-publics
23. Fishkin, J.S., Luskin, R.C., Jowell, R.: Deliberative polling and public consultation. Parliam. Aff. **53**(4), 657–666 (2000). https://doi.org/10.1093/pa/53.4.657
24. Flood, R.L., Romm, N.: Contours of diversity management and triple loop learning. Kybernetes **25**(7/8), 154–163 (1996)
25. Gerlich, M.: Ai tools in society: impacts on cognitive offloading and the future of critical thinking. Societies **15**(1), 6 (2025). https://www.mdpi.com/2075-4698/15/1/6
26. Gilens, M., Page, B.I.: Testing theories of american politics: elites, interest groups, and average citizens. Perspect. Polit. **12**(3), 564–581 (2014). https://doi.org/10.1017/S1537592714001595
27. Graber, J.: Algorithmic choice (2023). https://bsky.social/about/blog/3-30-2023-algorithmic-choice
28. Habermas, J.: The Theory of Communicative Action (Lifeworld and System: A Critique of Functionalist Reason), vol. 2. Beacon Press, Boston (1987)
29. Heath, J.: Communicative Action and Rational Choice. MIT Press, Cambridge, MA (2001)
30. Higgins, E.: Global nature of information disorder (2025). https://www.jbs.cam.ac.uk/events/cambridge-disinformation-summit-2025
31. High, T.: The canonical debate (2018). https://github.com/canonical-debate-lab/paper/blob/master/README.mediawiki
32. Ito, T., Hadfi, R., Suzuki, S.: An agent that facilitates crowd discussion. Group Decis. Negot. **31**, 621 – 647 (2021). https://api.semanticscholar.org/CorpusID:243839643

33. Jeantet, D., Savarese, M.: Brazilian city enacts an ordinance that was secretly written by chatgpt (2023). https://apnews.com/article/brazil-artificial-intelligence-porto-alegre-5afd1240afe7b6ac202bb0bbc45e08d4
34. Kahneman, D., Tversky, A.: On the reality of cognitive illusions. Psychol. Rev. **103**(3), 582–91 (1996). https://doi.org/10.1037/0033-295X.103.3.582, discussion 592–6
35. Kerr, D.: Musk's ai grok bot rants about 'white genocide' in South Africa in unrelated chats. The Guardian (2025). https://www.theguardian.com/technology/2025/may/14/elon-musk-grok-white-genocide
36. Kirschner, P.A., Buckingham Shum, S.J., Carr, C.S. (eds.): Visualizing Argumentation. Springer-Verlag, London (2003). http://www.visualizingargumentation.info/
37. Kosmyna, N., et al.: Your brain on chatgpt: Accumulation of cognitive debt when using an ai assistant for essay writing task (2025). https://arxiv.org/abs/2506.08872
38. Maturana, H., Varela, F.: Autopoiesis and Cognition. Boston Studies in the Philosophy of Science, D. Reidel, Boston (1980)
39. Mercier, H., Sperber, D.: The Enigma of Reason. Harvard University Press, Cambridge, MA, USA (2017)
40. Mouffe, C.: Agonistics: Thinking the World Politically. Verso Books, New York, NY (2013)
41. Ovadya, A., et al.: Democratic ai is possible. the democracy levels framework shows how it might work (2025). https://arxiv.org/abs/2411.09222
42. Parent, M.A.: Towards knowledge federation. In: Hegeland, F. (ed.) The Future of Text, vol. V, pp. 188–190. Future Text Publishing (2024). https://futuretextpublishing.com/vol-5/
43. Parent, M.A., Grégoire, B.: Architecture and cross-platform interoperability specification. Technical report, Catalyst (2014). http://bit.ly/catalyst_interop3
44. Parent, M.A., de Liddo, A., Klein, M., Ullman, T.: Project testbed: argument mapping & deliberation analytics. Tech. rep., Catalyst (2015). http://catalyst-fp7.eu/wp-content/uploads/2016/01/CATALYST_WP4_D4.2b.pdf
45. Parent, M.A., Park, J.: Sensecraft game design (2023). http://bit.ly/4l9Bl8U, https://docs.google.com/presentation/d/1K60P4xFMt9v7X9eDjkQTPfFJqQGDbss9CzoOGPlDkMA/edit#slide=id.p
46. Parsons, T.: The Structure of Social Action. McGrawHill, New York (1937)
47. Popper, K.: The Open Society and Its Enemies, vol. 1. Routledge (1945)
48. Rawls, J.: The idea of an overlapping consensus. Oxf. J. Leg. Stud. **7**, 251–276 (1988)
49. Samons, L.: What's Wrong with Democracy?: From Athenian Practice to American Worship. University of California Press (2004)
50. Schelling, T.C.: The Strategy of Conflict. Oxford University Press, New York (1963)
51. Schneier, B.: How ai will change democracy (2024). https://www.schneier.com/blog/archives/2024/05/how-ai-will-change-democracy.html
52. Snowden, D., Boone, M.: A leader's framework for decision making. Harvard Bus. Rev. **85**, 68–76, 149 (2007)
53. Tessler, M.H., et al.: Ai can help humans find common ground in democratic deliberation. Science **386**(6719), eadq2852 (2024). https://www.science.org/doi/abs/10.1126/science.adq2852
54. Tetlock, P.E.: Expert Political Judgment: How Good Is It? How Can We Know? Princeton University Press (2005)

55. Tosey, P., Visser, M., Saunders, M.: The origins and conceptualizations of 'triple-loop' learning: A critical review. Manage. Learn. **43**, 291–307 (2012). https://doi.org/10.1177/1350507611426239
56. Walton, D., Reed, C., Macagno, F.: Argumentation Schemes. Cambridge University Press, Cambridge (2008)
57. Warden, J., Nakayama, J., Dietze, F.: The global brain algorithm (2024). https://social-protocols.org/global-brain/
58. Weber, M.: The Protestant Ethic and the Spirit of Capitalism. Charles Scribner's Sons, New York (1958)
59. Weidinger, L., et al.: Ethical and social risks of harm from language models (2021).https://arxiv.org/abs/2112.04359
60. Wille, R.: Restructuring lattice theory: An approach based on hierarchies of concepts. In: Rival, I. (ed.) Ordered Sets, pp. 445–470. Springer, Netherlands, Dordrecht (1982)
61. Yuan, Z., Cheng, X.D.Y.: Impact of media dependence: how emotional interactions between users and chat robots affect human socialization? Front. Psychol. **15**, 1664–1078 (2024). https://doi.org/10.3389/fpsyg.2024.1388860

LLMs in Court: Risks and Governance of LLMs in Judicial Decision-Making

Djallel Bouneffouf[1(✉)] and Sara Migliorini[2]

[1] IBM Thomas J. Watson Research Center, New York, USA
djallel.bouneffouf@ibm.com
[2] Faculty of Law, University of Macau, Macau, China
saramigliorini@um.edu.mo

Abstract. Large language models (LLMs) are rapidly entering judicial workflows, assisting with research, summarization, and drafting. Yet their unverified use by judges risks undermining core tenets of legal legitimacy: accountability, consistency, and transparency. This paper empirically demonstrates interpretive divergence across leading LLMs (GPT-4, Claude, Gemini, LLaMA) on benchmarked legal tasks, revealing systematic vulnerabilities we classify as omission, injection, and framing loopholes. Using controlled prompt perturbations, semantic embedding comparisons, and cross-model evaluations on CaseHOLD and LexGLUE, we quantify semantic drift and show how minor prompt variations and model design choices materially affect legal conclusions. We argue that these dynamics, if LLMs are deployed without safeguard, will erode due process and public trust in the judiciary. Drawing on insights from judicial behavior literature, we propose a governance framework: multi-model deliberation, independent auditing and certification, and domain-specific validation protocols. Our roadmap aims to ensure LLM assistance augments, rather than undermines, the fairness and legitimacy of judicial decision-making.

Keywords: LLM · Judicial decision making · Governance

1 Introduction

The integration of large language models (LLMs) such as GPT-4, Claude, and LLaMA into legal workflows introduces a novel set of epistemological and procedural challenges for the justice system. These models, trained on vast corpora that include legal texts, statutes, and case law, have demonstrated remarkable competence in tasks ranging from legal summarization to precedent retrieval and even argument generation [Hendrycks *et al.*, 2020]. However, their utility in high-stakes environments like courts and legal advice is tempered by foundational uncertainties in how they interpret and apply legal information.

Although LLMs can be configured to behave deterministically (e.g., with fixed seeds and top-1 sampling), their typical deployment introduces stochasticity, through temperature settings or top k sampling, to enhance creativity or diversity. In legal applications, this stochasticity, though intentional, can introduce interpretive instability, especially when prompt sensitivity is not well understood. Thus, while not a core

J. Haqbeen et al. (Eds.): IJCAI 2025, LNAI 16400, pp. 48–59, 2026.
https://doi.org/10.1007/978-981-95-9667-6_4

architectural constraint, non-determinism as deployed remains a significant operational risk. The same legal question, posed with minor variations in the wording or phrasing, can elicit substantively different interpretations from the same model instance [Thakur, 2024]. Such prompt sensitivity raises fundamental concerns about consistency, reproducibility, and transparency, three pillars of due process in legal decision-making. In adversarial settings such as litigation, the ability of LLMs to offer subtly divergent interpretations could be strategically exploited, effectively creating "algorithmic loopholes" that undermine equitable outcomes.

Recent benchmarking efforts using curated legal datasets—such as the CaseHOLD dataset for legal entailment [Zheng *et al.*, 2021] and the LexGLUE benchmark suite for legal natural language understanding [Chalkidis *et al.*, 2021]—have further illustrated the extent to which even the most advanced LLMs vary in their legal reasoning capabilities. These discrepancies are not limited to factual interpretation or logical consistency; they extend into deep normative principles.

This paper seeks to systematically explore the interpretive divergence among state-of-the-art LLMs when applied to legal reasoning tasks. We introduce a multi-layered evaluation framework that combines controlled simulations, prompt perturbation experiments, and quantitative semantic comparisons. Of particular interest is the tendency of different LLMs to introduce distinct statutory or case-based justifications for similar conclusions. This effect not only reveals internal inconsistencies but also introduces epistemic opacity into the decision-making pipeline, especially when such suggestions are presented to judges or clerks as ostensibly neutral recommendations.

We demonstrate how interpretive drift among LLMs can result in materially different outcomes in different scenarios. Our results underscore the urgency of developing regulatory standards, interpretive alignment protocols, and rigorous validation procedures before LLMs can be safely and responsibly integrated into judicial and legal support systems.

2 Related Work

The intersection of artificial intelligence and law has attracted growing scholarly attention, particularly as large language models (LLMs) become more proficient in legal reasoning tasks. Early work in this domain focused on rule-based expert systems for legal reasoning [Sergot *et al.*, 1986], but the advent of deep learning has significantly expanded the scope of computational legal analysis.

Recent benchmarks such as CASEHOLD [Zheng *et al.*, 2021], LEGALBENCH [Guha *et al.*, 2023] and LEXGLUE [Chalkidis *et al.*, 2021] have provided standardized data sets for evaluating LLM in tasks such as legal entailment, prediction of case outcomes, and statute retrieval. These resources have revealed the capabilities and limitations of transformer-based models like GPT-3 and GPT-4 in handling complex legal texts.

Studies have also documented the susceptibility of LLMs to prompt engineering and framing biases, which can lead to divergent outputs for semantically equivalent inputs [Thakur, 2024; Liang *et al.*, 2022]. Such variability is particularly concerning in legal contexts, where interpretive stability is a normative requirement. Some works have examined this issue in the context of AI transparency and alignment [Marcus and Davis, 2020; Liu *et al.*, 2023], raising questions about the reliability of LLMs in decision-support roles.

A growing body of literature has explored the implications of using AI in judicial or quasi-judicial settings. For example, [Surden, 2018] discusses the limits of automation in legal decision-making, emphasizing that while AI may assist with tasks such as legal search and summarization, it lacks the moral and institutional accountability required of judges. Similarly, [Corbett-Davies *et al.*, 2017] raises concerns about due process and algorithmic opacity in legal automation.

Despite these advances, few works have systematically investigated how divergences in LLM legal interpretation may introduce or amplify legal loopholes. Our study contributes to this gap by empirically analyzing interpretive variability across LLMs and exploring the risks that models fabricate or misattribute statutory or case-based foundations.

3 Methodology

Our goal is to investigate whether large language models (LLMs) produce divergent legal interpretations from the same source texts, potentially leading to exploitable legal loopholes. To achieve this, we follow a multi-stage evaluation framework that combines document parsing, semantic comparison.

As illustrated in Fig. 1, the diagram depicts the sequential and interdependent structure of the evaluation pipeline. Specifically:

3.1 Model Selection

We select a range of state-of-the-art LLMs for evaluation, including proprietary models such as GPT-4 (OpenAI), Claude (Anthropic), and Gemini (Google DeepMind), as well as open-source models such as LLaMA 3 [Touvron *et al.*, 2023] and Mistral [Karamcheti *et al.*, 2021]. These models represent diverse training corpora, prompting behavior, and alignment strategies.

This framework enables us to assess not only raw accuracy but also epistemic stability and risk of misuse.

3.2 Dataset

We employ two primary datasets:

- **CaseHOLD** [Zheng *et al.*, 2021]: A multiple-choice dataset requiring identification of correct legal holdings for case summaries.
- **LexGLUE** [Chalkidis *et al.*, 2021]: A benchmark for legal NLU tasks such as statute classification, entailment, and contract clause matching.

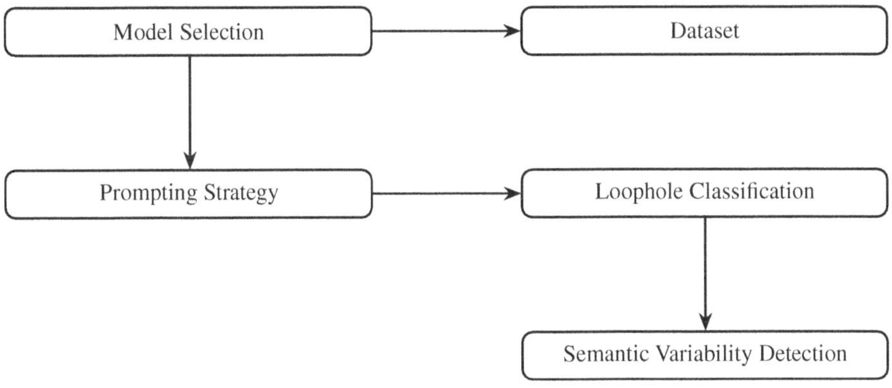

Fig. 1. Overview of the experimental setup.

3.3 Prompting Strategy

Each legal text is processed using zero-shot and few-shot prompting techniques across all models. We design prompts to simulate judicial reasoning (e.g., "Act as a judge interpreting this clause..."), client-side consultation, and statute interpretation tasks. We systematically vary the prompt framing to evaluate model sensitivity to language perturbations.

3.4 Semantic Variability Detection

To quantify interpretive variability, we employ **sentence embedding similarity**. Specifically, we use `Sentence-BERT` [Reimers and Gurevych, 2019] to generate vector representations of model outputs and compute cosine similarity scores. This approach allows us to assess the semantic alignment of interpretations produced by different LLMs when responding to the same legal input.

3.5 Loophole Classification

As large language models (LLMs) are increasingly integrated into legal decision-support systems, a growing concern is the emergence of systematic interpretive failures that we term *loopholes*. These are not bugs in the software per se, but rather predictable divergences from legally sound reasoning patterns, often influenced by model limitations, prompt framing, or insufficient legal grounding. We propose a tripartite classification of such LLM-induced loopholes, drawing from recent legal NLP and generative AI literature.

- **Omission Loopholes**: These occur when an LLM fails to reference, apply, or even acknowledge relevant legal provisions, principles, or precedents that are germane to a case. Such omissions may stem from limitations in context length, poor prompt design, or the model's inadequate understanding of domain-specific legal entailments. Prior studies have demonstrated that even specialized legal models frequently miss case-specific holdings or controlling statutes in benchmark datasets like CaseHOLD and LexGLUE [Zheng *et al.*, 2021].

- **Injection Loopholes**: These involve the generation of legally irrelevant statutes, cases, or doctrinal principles. Unlike mere factual inaccuracies, injection loopholes represent a deeper epistemic risk: the attribution of legal authority to hallucinated content. This phenomenon has been observed in closed and open source LLMs, where references to non-existent court decisions or fabricated codes are offered as authoritative justifications [Thakur, 2024]. Such outputs may mislead non-expert users or propagate false legal reasoning in downstream workflows.
- **Framing Loopholes**: These reflect the sensitivity of LLM outputs to subtle variations in prompt wording, legal context, or question structure. Two logically equivalent queries may yield materially different interpretations or conclusions due to framing effects. Recent prompt engineering research has shown that even high-performing models such as GPT-4 and Claude exhibit significant variability in their legal reasoning when prompt phrasing is modified [Thakur, 2024]. These loopholes pose risks in adversarial settings, such as litigation, where prompt manipulation could strategically influence an LLM's response.

Together, these categories capture a spectrum of vulnerabilities in the interpretive behavior of legal LLMs. Identifying and systematizing them is a critical step toward developing robust benchmarks, safety guidelines, and governance standards for AI in law.

The arrow from *Model Selection* to *Prompting Strategy* reflects how the capabilities and limitations of a given language model (e.g., GPT-4, Claude, LLaMA) inform the design of the prompting approach, such as zero-shot or few-shot configurations, tailored to the architecture and instruction follow-up behavior of that model.

The connection from *Model Selection* to *Dataset* highlights that the choice of model may also influence which legal datasets are best suited for evaluation. For example, models with stronger pre-training in legal corpora may perform differently in data sets such as CaseHOLD [Zheng *et al.*, 2021] or LexGLUE [Chalkidis *et al.*, 2021].

The transition from *Prompting Strategy* to *Loophole Classification* denotes that the nature of the prompt (e.g. explicit legal questions, implicit reasoning tasks) affects how potential legal loopholes, such as omissions, hallucinated references or divergences based on framing, are surfaced and classified.

Finally, the arrow from *Loophole Classification* to *Semantic Variability Detection* captures the subsequent analytical stage in which the identified loopholes are examined through semantic similarity metrics (e.g., using Sentence-BERT embeddings) to assess interpretive drift or inconsistency across model outputs.

3.6 Visualization and Metrics

We report:

- Con consistency of cross-model interpretation using cosine similarity matrices.
- Loophole prevalence rates per model and per prompt template.

4 Results

This section presents the results of our comparative evaluation across four LLMs: GPT-4, Claude 3, Gemini 1.5, and LLaMA 3. We evaluated interpretive variability, the types of loopholes identified, and prompt sensitivity.

4.1 Semantic Variability

For the Semantic Variability experiment (as referenced in Table 1), we used a curated subset of the CaseHOLD dataset [Zheng *et al.*, 2021], which consists of U.S. court case holdings designed to test a model's ability to perform legal reasoning. Specifically:

We selected 50 legal prompts from CaseHOLD that involve statutory interpretation, precedent application, and intent analysis.

Each prompt was submitted to four different LLMs: GPT-4, Claude, Gemini, and LLaMA.

The LLM outputs were encoded using Sentence-BERT to obtain vector representations.

We then calculated pairwise cosine similarity between embeddings to quantify divergence.

Table 1. Mean Cosine Similarity Between Model Interpretations

	GPT-4	Claude 3	Gemini 1.5	LLaMA 3
GPT-4	1.00	0.87	0.81	0.76
Claude 3	0.87	1.00	0.83	0.74
Gemini 1.5	0.81	0.83	1.00	0.69
LLaMA 3	0.76	0.74	0.69	1.00

Table 1 reports the average pairwise cosine similarity between model-generated interpretations of identical legal inputs. These values serve as a proxy for semantic alignment across different large language models (LLMs). As expected, diagonal entries reflect perfect self-similarity (1.00). Notably, GPT-4 and Claude 3 exhibit the highest cross-model alignment (0.87), followed by GPT-4 and Gemini 1.5 (0.81), suggesting that closed-source models tend to produce more consistent interpretations. In contrast, LLaMA 3 consistently yields the lowest similarity scores with other models (e.g., 0.69 with Gemini 1.5 and 0.74 with Claude 3), indicating greater semantic divergence. These findings point to underlying architectural and training differences that influence legal interpretability. The observed variance has important implications for the deployment of LLMs in legal applications, where consistency and reliability are paramount.

4.2 Loophole Frequency

Figure 2 illustrates the upper bound percentage of legal loopholes per LLM. In these experiments, we have used GPT-4 as the evaluator. Here we prompt it to check for different types of loophole.

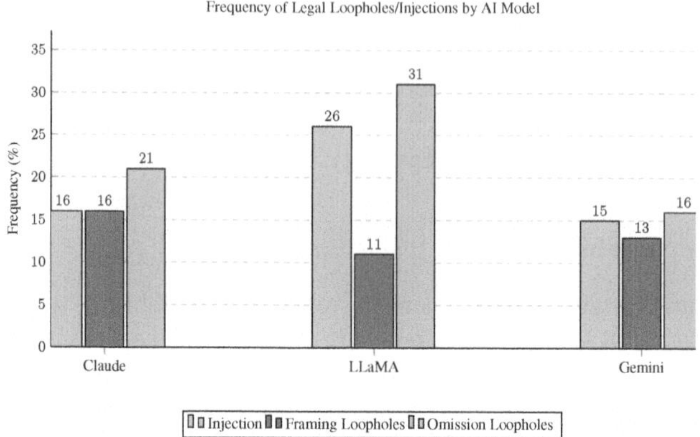

Fig. 2. Comparative analysis of loophole frequencies across AI models. *Note: Omission loopholes dominate in all models, especially where statutory context is sparse.*

Key findings:

- **Injection** was higher in LLaMA 3, suggesting hallucinated references to statutes or cases.
- **Framing Loopholes** occurred more frequently in Claude when prompt phrasing was subtly modified.
- **Omission Loopholes** were widespread in all models, particularly when statutory context was sparse.

4.3 Prompt Sensitivity Analysis

We generated multiple paraphrased versions of the same legal prompt from the CaseHOLD dataset [Zheng *et al.*, 2021]. Each paraphrase preserved the original legal meaning but varied in syntactic structure, tone, or framing. For each paraphrased prompt, we collected outputs from four LLMs (GPT-4, Claude, Gemini, LLaMA).

We then used `Sentence-BERT` [Reimers and Gurevych, 2019] to compute cosine similarity between the base response and responses to paraphrased prompts. A significant drop in cosine similarity (below a predefined threshold of 0.85) was interpreted as semantic drift—indicating that the LLM produced meaningfully different interpretations of the same legal issue.

The *Drift Rate (%)* column in Table 2 quantifies how often each LLM produced materially different legal interpretations in response to semantically equivalent, but differently worded, prompts. We observe that prompt rewording led to a significant semantic drift in 23% of model output, with Claude and LLama showing the highest variability.

5 Discussion

Our findings highlight that while large language models (LLMs) can process legal documents with high fluency and surface coherence, their interpretive variability introduces

Table 2. Semantic Drift Rate

Model	Drift Rate (%)
GPT-4	24.0 ± 6.1
Claude 3	26.6 ± 3.5
Gemini 1.5	18.0 ± 4.1
LLaMA 3	26.3 ± 5.3
Mean	**23.72**

significant risks in contexts requiring precision and consistency, such as judicial or legislative applications. Differences in interpretation, especially in edge cases, suggest that LLMs do not share a stable internal representation of legal concepts, which can be exploited as *algorithmic loopholes*.

Injection: One of the most concerning phenomena observed was that LLMs introduced irrelevant legal precedents and statutes. While hallucination is a known issue in language models, its appearance in legal reasoning carries higher stakes, as it may mislead users or judges who rely on such models for advisory or assistant tasks.

Prompt Sensitivity: Even slight modifications in prompt language led to different legal conclusions, especially for higher-order reasoning tasks. This sensitivity raises concerns about model robustness and opens the door to adversarial prompting, where users may steer models toward desired outcomes.

6 A Roadmap for the Adoption of LLMs in Judicial Settings

Research into judicial decision-making is a paramount element of proposals for reforms that target the judiciary in a view to minimize the identified shortcomings [Posner, 2010; Banks and O'Brien, 2015]. Building on our results, we discuss how to integrate the use of LLMs into judicial settings, aiming to support judges in their decision-making processes and ultimately enhance trust in the judiciary.

To achieve this, we position our research within the broader body of existing literature in law and social sciences, which has extensively examined judicial behaviour and public trust in the judicial system. We then put forward proposals that contribute to leverage LLMs to overcome existing and previously identified shortcomings of the current judicial decision-making process.

6.1 Judicial Behaviour and Trust in the Judiciary

Public trust in the judiciary is directly tied to the perceived fairness and accuracy of judicial decision-making. The judicial system requires public confidence to maintain its legitimacy and function effectively [Tyler, 2006]. Research indicates that trust in the judiciary correlates not only with broader institutional credibility [Liu and Chen, 2020], but crucially also with perceived procedural justice, which can go as far as to "attenuate the negative impact of unfavourable decisions often made by judges in courtrooms" [Grootelaar and van den Bos, 2018]. While occasional mistakes might be tolerated, systematic errors in judicial decision-making erode this trust [Guthrie *et al.*, 2000], as fairness in both process and outcome is paramount for institutional legitimacy [Grootelaar and van den Bos, 2018].

However, despite the ideal of impartiality, judicial decision-making is subject to human limitations and external influences. Classic legal formalism assumes that judges apply rules to facts in a rational, mechanical manner, yet legal realism highlights the significant role of human factors in shaping judicial outcomes [Epstein, 2014]. Judges, like all humans, are vulnerable to all sorts of limitations and biases that can distort their reasoning [Harris and Sen, 2019; Rachlinski and Wistrich, 2017a]. These biases are further compounded by the inherent complexity of cases: litigation frequently involves conflicting factual accounts and broad legal principles, which leave significant room for interpretation [Priest and Klein, 1984], or require complex, multifactorial assessment that judges may tend to unconsciously simplify [Levy, 2013; Beebe, 2006].

Empirical research highlights the significant impact of extraneous variables on judicial decision-making, challenging the ideal of impartial adjudication. For example, a study examining the common caricature of legal realism—summed up by the phrase "justice is what the judge had for breakfast"—found that judicial decisions in parole cases were influenced by the time of day. Specifically, the likelihood of favorable rulings declined steadily as sessions progressed but rebounded following breaks [Danziger *et al.*, 2011]. Furthermore, although judges tend to score higher than the general population in measures of reasoning and decision-making, they remain susceptible to heuristics and cognitive biases [Bystranowski *et al.*, 2021; Rachlinski and Wistrich, 2017b; Guthrie *et al.*, 2007].

Judicial decision-making is also greatly influenced by both intrinsic and systemic biases, shaped by individual perspectives and institutional factors. Realist, critical, and feminist scholars highlight how personal characteristics and interests impact judges' behavior [Harris and Sen, 2019; Rachlinski andWistrich, 2017a]. The selection mechanisms and incentives of judges seem to further shape their behavior [Posner, 2010]. Furthermore, certain aspects of judicial procedures are inherently linked to shortcomings in judicial decision-making. Prosecutorial recommendations [Rachlinski and Wistrich, 2017a; Englich, 2006] and evidence presented to judges, including inadmissible evidence, may significantly influence judicial outcomes [Wistrich *et al.*, 2004].

Corrective mechanisms such as collegiality, accountability, and diversity on the bench play a critical role in improving the quality and perceived fairness of judicial decision-making. Collegiality, which arises from the collaborative nature of multi-member judicial panels, helps mitigate judges' ideological preferences and enables courts to reach better decisions [Edwards, 2003]. The accountability created by peer scrutiny and the potential for higher court review motivates judges to carefully consider their rulings [Schanzenbach and Tiller, 2005]. Finally, the presence of non-homogeneous members on the bench has also been shown to lead to better outcomes [Boyd *et al.*, 2010]. For example, the presence of a minority judge has been found to positively influence the perspectives of other panel members, even in cases not related to the specific background or characteristics of the minority judge [Kastellec, 2013; Peresie, 2004].

6.2 Proposals for Integrating LLMs Into Judicial Decision-Making to Foster Trust

Integrating LLMs into judicial decision-making offers a transformative opportunity to reduce biases and enhance public trust. However, their adoption should be gradual and targeted to preserve balance and ensure that final accountability for decisions remains with human judges. While judges face intense public and academic scrutiny, often exaggerating systemic flaws, the judiciary in many jurisdictions remains fundamentally trusted and resilient. To address persistent challenges while upholding transparency and fairness, we propose the following strategies:

- Multiple models should be employed in parallel to cross-validate interpretations. This approach, feasible with existing technology, could improve decision making by fostering the benefits of collegiality and diversity, even in cases decided by a single judge.
- Legal LLMs should undergo transparent audits conducted by independent third parties. A certification mechanism could be implemented to detect and flag outputs indicative of potential loophole generation, allowing human judges to independently assess and verify such instances.

These strategies should also be adapted to the specific procedural requirements of each jurisdiction.

7 Conclusion

This study demonstrates that large language models exhibit interpretive divergence when analyzing legal texts, and that this divergence may give rise to systematic vulnerabilities—what we term *AI-induced legal loopholes*. These findings point to the need for caution in using LLMs for high-stakes decision making, especially in domains such as law, where interpretive precision is paramount.

Future work should focus on developing robust metrics for semantic consistency, training models explicitly on comparative case law reasoning, and integrating human-in-the-loop systems to verify and contextualize LLM outputs before they are deployed in judicial decision making. In addition, further work should assess the potential for synthetic collegiality to address the well-known biases and shortcoming of judicial decision making.

References

Banks, C.P., O'Brien, D.M.: The judicial process: Law, courts, and judicial politics. CQ Press (2015)

Beebe, B.: An empirical study of the multifactor tests for trademark infringement. Calif. Law Rev. **94**, 61581–654 (2006)

Boyd, C.L., Epstein, L., Martin, A.D.: Untangling the causal effects of sex on judging. Am. J. Polit. Sci. **54**, 389–411 (2010)

Bystranowski, P., Janik, B., Próchnicki, M., Skórska, P.: Anchoring effect in legal decision-making: a meta-analysis. Law Hum Behav. **45**(1), 1 (2021)

Chalkidis, I., et al.: LexGLUE: A benchmark dataset for legal language understanding in English. *arXiv preprint*arXiv:2110.00976 (2021)

Corbett-Davies, S., Pierson, E., Feller, A., Goel, S., Huq, A.: Algorithmic decision making and the cost of fairness. In: Proceedings of the 23rd ACM SIGKDD International Conference on Knowledge Discovery and Data Mining, pp. 797–806 (2017)

Danziger, S., Levav, J., Avnaim-Pesso, L.: Extraneous factors in judicial decisions. Proc. Natl. Acad. Sci. **108**(17), 6889–6892 (2011)

Edwards, H.T.: The effects of collegiality on judicial decision making. Univ. Pa. Law Rev. **151**(5), 1639–1690 (2003)

Englich, B.: Blind or biased? Justitia's susceptibility to anchoring effects in the courtroom based on given numerical representations. Law Policy **28**(4), 497–514 (2006)

Epstein, D.Z.: Rationality, legitimacy, and the law. Washington University Jurisprudence Review **7**, 1 (2014)

Grootelaar, H.A.M., van den Bos, K.: How litigants in Dutch courtrooms come to trust judges: the role of perceived procedural justice, outcome favorability, and other sociolegal moderators. Law Soc. Rev. **52**(1), 234–268 (2018)

Guha, N., et al.: LegalBench: a collaboratively built benchmark for measuring legal reasoning in large language models. Adv. Neural. Inf. Process. Syst. **36**, 44123–44279 (2023)

Guthrie, C., Rachlinski, J.J., Wistrich, A.J.: Inside the judicial mind. Cornell Law Rev. **86**, 777 (2000)

Guthrie, C., Rachlinski, J.J., Wistrich, A.J.: Blinking on the bench: how judges decide cases. Cornell Law Rev. **93**, 11–43 (2007)

Harris, A., Sen, M.: Bias and judging. Annu. Rev. Polit. Sci. **22**, 241–259 (2019)

Hendrycks, D., et al.: Measuring massive multitask language understanding. arXiv preprint arXiv:2009.03300 (2020)

Karamcheti, S., et al.: Mistral-a journey towards reproducible language model training, Tatsunori Hashimoto (2021)

Kastellec, J.P.: Racial diversity and judicial influence on appellate courts. Am. J. Polit. Sci. **57**(1), 167–183 (2013)

Levy, M.K.: Judging the flood of litigation. Univ. Chicago Law Rev. 1007–1077 (2013)

Liang, W., et al.: Advances, challenges and opportunities in creating data for trustworthy AI. Nat. Mach. Intell. **4**(8), 669–677 (2022)

Liu, J.Z., Chen, L.: Jury trial and public trust in the judiciary: evidence from cross-countries comparison. Asia Pacific Law Rev. **28**(2), 412–436 (2020)

Liu, Y., et al.: Trustworthy LLMs: a survey and guideline for evaluating large language models' alignment. arXiv preprint arXiv:2308.05374 (2023)

Marcus, G., Davis, E.: GPT-3, bloviator: OpenAI's language generator has no idea what it's talking about. Technol. Rev. **294** (2020)

Peresie, J.L.: Female judges matter: gender and collegial decision making in the federal appellate courts. Yale LJ **114**, 1759 (2004)

Posner, R.A.: How judges think. Harvard University Press (2010)

Priest, G.L., Klein, B.: The selection of disputes for litigation. J. Legal Stud. **13**(1), 1–55 (1984)

Rachlinski, J.J., Wistrich, A.J.: Judging the judiciary by the numbers: empirical research on judges. Ann. Rev. Law Soc. Sci. **13**, 203–229 (2017)

Rachlinski, J.J., Wistrich, A.J.: Judging the judiciary by the numbers: Empirical research on judges. Ann. Rev. Law Soc. Sci. **13**(1), 203–229 (2017)

Reimers, N., Gurevych, I.: Sentence-BERT: Sentence embeddings using Siamese BERT-networks. arXiv preprint arXiv:1908.10084 (2019)

Schanzenbach, M.M., Tiller, E.: Strategic judging under the united states sentencing guidelines: instrument choice theory and evidence. In: American Law & Economics Association Annual Meetings, pp. 12. bepress (2005)

Sergot, M.J., Sadri, F., Kowalski, R.A., Kriwaczek, F., Hammond, P., Cory, H.T.: The British nationality act as a logic program. Commun. ACM **29**(5), 370–386 (1986)

Surden, H.: Artificial intelligence and law: an overview. Ga. St. UL Rev. **35**, 1305 (2018)

Thakur, A.: The art of prompting: Unleashing the power of large language models (2024)

Touvron, H., et al.: Llama: Open and efficient foundation language models. arXiv preprint arXiv:2302.13971 (2023)

Tom, R.: Tyler. Princeton University Press, Why people obey the law (2006)

Wistrich, A.J., Guthrie, C., Rachlinski, J.J.: Can judges ignore inadmissible information-the difficulty of deliberately disregarding. U. Pa. L. Rev. **153**, 1251 (2004)

Zheng, L., Guha, N., Anderson, B.R., Henderson, P., Ho, D.E.: When does pretraining help? assessing self-supervised learning for law and the CaseHOLD dataset of 53,000+ legal holdings. In: Proceedings of the Eighteenth International Conference on Artificial Intelligence and Law, pp. 159–168 (2021)

The Effects of an AI Participant on Online Group Deliberation: Evidence from a Controlled Study with Afghan Youth

Takayuki Ito(✉) and Jawad Haqbeen

Kyoto University, Kyoto 606-8501, Japan
{ito,jawad.haqbeen}@i.kyoto-u.ac.jp

Abstract. This study investigates the effects of introducing a large language model (LLM)-based AI participant into online group discussions among Afghan youth. Through a controlled experiment, we compare groups with and without an AI interlocutor on multiple dimensions, including engagement, perceived usefulness, group dynamics, opinion change, and thematic discourse shifts. Results indicate that the AI participant significantly enhances perceived team fluidity and fosters more optimistic, technology-oriented dialogue, without diminishing human engagement or agency. These findings have implications for digital civic engagement, participatory policy design, and peacebuilding in fragile sociopolitical contexts.

Keywords: AI agents · Consensus · Discussion Support

1 Introduction

Recent advances in artificial intelligence, particularly large language models (LLMs), have inspired interest in enhancing group deliberation. AI agents can address challenges such as information overload, polarization, and facilitation bias. For example, studies show AI-driven mediators [2,3,5,6,8,9,11,16–18] effectively summarize diverse viewpoints, promoting clearer, more unbiased, and inclusive discussions. Early platforms like Polis and Remesh already demonstrate the potential of algorithmic agents to process real-time mass inputs, laying groundwork for interactive LLM-based participation [1,15].

The Afghan context [4,5,7,8,17] adds urgency and significance to using AI in deliberations. Due to decades of conflict, traditional civic dialogue remains dangerous or impractical, especially for marginalized groups such as women or ethnic minorities. Recent regime changes have further restricted civil liberties, exacerbating the need for safe online spaces. Despite these challenges, Afghan youth remain civically engaged, making AI-enhanced online deliberations a critical alternative for inclusive civic participation in an otherwise restrictive environment.

J. Haqbeen et al. (Eds.): IJCAI 2025, LNAI 16400, pp. 60–69, 2026.
https://doi.org/10.1007/978-981-95-9667-6_5

Introducing an AI participant involves important theoretical considerations. Social presence theory suggests AI agents capable of responsive and human-like interactions can be perceived as legitimate peers in conversations. This aligns with the Computers Are Social Actors (CASA) paradigm [14], which shows that humans naturally apply social behaviors to human-like AI. Consequently, AI participants may improve collective intelligence and shape group dynamics positively [11]. However, there are risks if humans overly rely on AI opinions, potentially undermining genuine dialogue.

This research builds on emerging empirical studies examining AI in civic participation. Previous experiments indicate that AI mediators foster greater consensus, improved clarity, and increased engagement. For instance, an AI mediator among UK citizens created more preferred summaries compared to humans, and similar studies in Afghanistan reported increased engagement and idea diversity due to conversational AI. Our study contributes uniquely by focusing specifically on Afghan youth, assessing whether observed benefits from AI involvement hold true in Afghanistan's challenging environment, and exploring new insights into human–AI dynamics in real-world deliberations.

2 Hyper-Democracy System

The architecture of the Hyper-democracy System is presented in Fig. 1. The system uses general web forum systems, including Discourse and D-Agree [11–13]. AI agents are implemented as Python programs and connected to Open AI's GPT4 using application programming interface (API). The Agent Manager manages multiple agents [10], monitoring the status on the discussion platform and overseeing interactions with the agents. All agents and the Agent Manager are running on Amazon Web Services (AWS) EC2 instances. In this paper, we use only one participant agent to verify the impact of an AI agent.

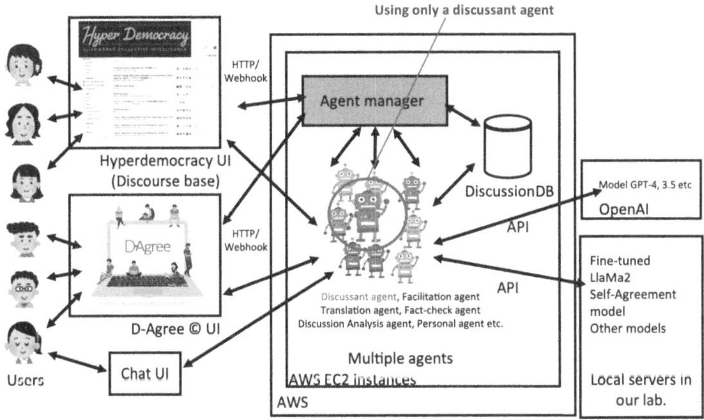

Fig. 1. The System Architecture.

3 Methods

3.1 Participants and Design

A total of eighty Afghan youth, aged between 18 and 39 years, participated in the study. The sample was gender-balanced and composed primarily of individuals with an undergraduate-level education. All participants demonstrated proficiency in English, ensuring effective communication during the discussions. Recruitment was conducted using a stratified sampling approach to ensure demographic diversity across gender and educational background.

Participants were randomly assigned to 20 discussion groups, each consisting of four members. These groups were then divided into two experimental conditions:

- **Batch 1 (Control, No AI):** Ten groups composed exclusively of four human participants. No AI was introduced in these discussions.
- **Batch 2 (Experimental, With AI):** Ten groups composed of three human participants and one AI participant, named "Anna." Anna was a large language model-based AI designed to engage as an equal participant in the group discussion. This configuration allowed for a direct comparison between purely human interactions and mixed human-AI deliberations.

3.2 Procedure

The experimental sessions were conducted over three consecutive days. Each group met online for structured discussion sessions facilitated through a designated digital platform.

- **Day 1:** Participants completed a pre-discussion survey that measured their expectations, prior experience with group discussions, and initial attitudes. This was followed by a five-hour online discussion where participants engaged with one another (and the AI in Batch 2) on a set of predetermined topics related to social challenges.
- **Day 2:** The discussions continued with a focus on refining ideas and exploring deeper viewpoints. Participants were encouraged to build upon arguments introduced on Day 1 and respond to others' contributions.
- **Day 3:** Final discussions were held, culminating in a wrap-up conversation and a post-discussion survey. This survey measured perceived outcomes, participant satisfaction, and reflection on any changes in personal opinions.

To ensure active engagement, a minimum participation threshold was enforced. All participants were required to post at least four contributions per hour. These posts could include original opinions, reactions to others' comments, or requests for clarification.

3.3 Measures

A mixed-method approach was used to assess the outcomes of the study.

- **Quantitative Measures:** Participants responded to a series of 5-point Likert scale items evaluating the following aspects:
  - Perceived usefulness of the discussion format and content
  - Ease of interaction with other participants (and with the AI, in Batch 2)
  - Expected and actual levels of participation
  - Degree of opinion change over the course of the discussion
- **Qualitative Measures:** The surveys also included open-ended questions that allowed participants to describe their experiences, reflections on group dynamics, and perceived impact of the AI (if applicable). This qualitative data provided deeper insights into the nature of the deliberations and the subjective value of the interaction.

This methodological design enabled a rigorous comparison of the group processes and outcomes in human-only versus human-AI group discussions.

4 Results

Perceived Usefulness of Discussion

Table 1. Perceived Usefulness: Pre- and Post-Discussion

Group	Pre: Effective/%	Post: Effective/%	AI Contribution (Batch 2)
No AI	78%	81%	—
With AI	73%	85%	83% rate AI as effective

Both experimental conditions (control and AI groups) positively evaluated the usefulness of the discussions. Notably, the AI group's rating for the usefulness of the discussion rose from 73% pre-discussion to 85% post-discussion, surpassing the control group's slight increase from 78% to 81%. Importantly, 83% of participants in the AI group explicitly rated the AI participant as effective, suggesting that the AI added substantial value to the dialogue (Tabel 1)

Participation and Engagement

Participation levels exceeded participants' initial expectations in both conditions, reflecting high engagement. Specifically, the control group displayed a median increase of 14 messages (from an expected 27 to an actual 41), slightly higher than the AI group's increase of 12 messages (from 24 to 36). Although both groups were highly engaged, the presence of the AI participant maintained robust human participation without evidence of crowding out human contributions (Table 2)

Table 2. Participation and Engagement

Group	Expected Messages (Median)	Actual Messages (Median)	Delta
No AI	27	41	+14
With AI	24	36	+12

Ease of Interaction

Table 3. Ease of Interaction (Post-Discussion)

Group	Agree/Strongly Agree (%)	Mann-Whitney U	*p*-value
No AI	86%	—	—
With AI	93%	602.0	0.029

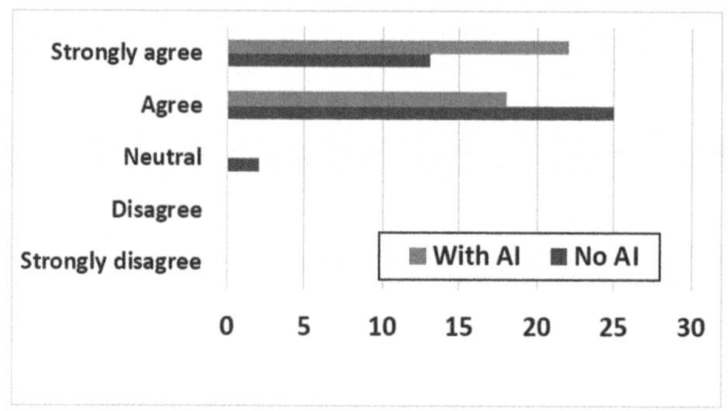

Fig. 2. Ease of Interaction (Post-Discussion).

Participants in the AI condition reported significantly improved ease of interaction, with 93% agreeing or strongly agreeing that interactions were smooth, compared to 86% in the control group. Statistical analysis confirmed this difference as significant (Mann-Whitney U = 602.0, p = 0.029). These findings suggest that the AI participant notably enhanced perceived team fluidity and communication ease (Table 3 and Fig. 2).

Degree of Opinion Change

Both conditions experienced opinion shifts during discussions, with slightly higher rates of opinion change in the AI condition (81% reported at least some change, with 23% reporting major changes) compared to the control condition (76% reported some change, with 18% major changes). However, these differences were not statistically significant (p = 0.804), indicating that while the AI contributed positively, it did not force convergence of opinions (see Table 4).

Table 4. Degree of Opinion Change

Group	At Least Some Change	Major Change	*p*-value
No AI	76%	18%	0.804
With AI	81%	23%	

Perceptions of the AI Participant (Batch 2 only)

Qualitative data underscored the supportive and non-dominating presence of the AI participant, Anna. Open-ended responses emphasized that Anna's contributions were constructive, enhancing dialogue without dominating discussions. Participants explicitly noted the AI's role in facilitating balanced interactions and fostering an inclusive atmosphere.

Thematic (Keyword) Analysis

Table 5. Most Frequent Post-Discussion Keywords and Thematic Shift

Group	Top Pre-discussion Keywords	Top Post-discussion Keywords
No AI	Taliban, education, online	Taliban, education, online, future
With AI	Taliban, technology	technology, good, alternative

A distinct thematic shift was observed in discussions with the AI participant. In contrast to control discussions, which largely retained initial topics (Taliban, education, online), AI-inclusive discussions exhibited a pronounced shift towards optimistic and solution-oriented keywords, prominently featuring terms such as 'technology,' 'good,' and 'alternative.' This shift suggests that the AI's presence helped guide discussions towards constructive, future-oriented perspectives (see Table 5)

Overall, these detailed findings highlight the beneficial impacts of integrating an AI participant into group deliberations, enhancing both interaction quality and thematic richness without diminishing human agency or participation (Table 6).

Statistical Analysis Overview

The statistical analyses provide insights into how the presence of an AI participant influenced online group discussions. Initially, both groups—those with and without AI—shared similar perceptions of the discussion's usefulness, indicated by a non-significant difference (Mann-Whitney U = 715.0, p = 0.363). This suggests that participants started from comparable expectations regarding the value of the discussions.

Table 6. Statistical Analysis Overview

Comparison	Mann-Whitney U	*p*-value	Interpretation
Perceived Usefulness (Pre)	715.0	0.363	Not significant
Ease of Interaction (Post)	602.0	0.029	Significant improvement
Opinion Change (Post)	775.0	0.804	Not significant

Following the discussions, a significant improvement was observed in the ease of interaction among participants in the AI condition compared to the control group (Mann-Whitney U = 602.0, p = 0.029). This indicates that the AI participant notably enhanced communication fluidity and facilitated smoother group interactions.

However, the presence of the AI participant did not significantly impact the degree of opinion change among participants (Mann-Whitney U = 775.0, p = 0.804). Although both groups reported shifts in their views during the discussions, the extent of these shifts did not differ meaningfully between the groups, suggesting that the AI's influence was supportive rather than directive in altering opinions.

5 Discussion

Our experiment provides empirical evidence that an LLM-based AI participant can enhance the fluidity, optimism, and perceived quality of group deliberation without crowding out human agency or engagement. The presence of the AI stimulated broader, more future-oriented conversation and was valued as a constructive peer, not an intrusive force. These effects were robust even in a culturally sensitive, politically fraught context.

This study contributes to the growing literature on human–AI collaboration in deliberative contexts. Prior research has examined AI as facilitators or summarizers, but our findings extend the *Computers Are Social Actors* (CASA) paradigm by demonstrating that participants accept AI not only as a tool but also as a legitimate peer. The AI's ability to shift discussions thematically toward optimism and technology-oriented solutions indicates that LLM-based agents can shape discursive frames in ways comparable to human participants, thereby enriching collective intelligence.

The practical implications span multiple domains:

- **Civic technology:** AI can foster inclusion and idea generation in marginalized settings, particularly in fragile states where civic dialogue is otherwise constrained. Deploying AI peers may reduce barriers for groups excluded from conventional forums.
- **Educational platforms:** The constructive presence of an AI participant suggests applications in online classrooms and peer-learning environments, where AI can stimulate creativity and broaden perspectives without diminishing students' voices.

- **Peacebuilding and policy design:** In politically sensitive contexts like Afghanistan, AI may help sustain dialogue that emphasizes constructive, future-oriented themes, potentially mitigating polarization and creating safer deliberative spaces.

Despite the positive outcomes, integrating AI participants raises critical ethical concerns. Transparency regarding AI identity is essential to avoid deception or over-reliance on algorithmic outputs. Additionally, while our results showed no evidence of opinion manipulation, the possibility of subtle agenda-setting effects must be monitored. Ethical deployment requires safeguards against bias in training data, mechanisms for accountability, and respect for cultural sensitivities in fragile environments.

Several limitations warrant acknowledgment. First, the study was conducted with Afghan youth fluent in English; results may not generalize to older demographics or non-English contexts. Second, the controlled design may not capture the complexities of large-scale, organically evolving deliberations. Third, the AI agent was restricted to one persona ("Anna"); variations in tone, style, or transparency of AI behavior might produce different outcomes. Finally, while thematic shifts were observed, longer-term impacts on sustained civic engagement remain unexplored.

Building on these findings, future work should explore:

- Scaling experiments to larger, multilingual populations to assess generalizability.
- Comparing different AI roles (peer vs. facilitator vs. summarizer) and levels of transparency.
- Investigating longitudinal effects on trust, agency, and civic efficacy when AI participants are repeatedly integrated into discussions.
- Developing normative frameworks for evaluating when and how AI participation enhances, rather than undermines, democratic processes.

Taken together, our results suggest that LLM-based AI participants can meaningfully contribute to civic dialogue, provided that their design and deployment remain ethically grounded and context-sensitive. This work lays a foundation for reimagining digital deliberation in fragile contexts and advancing the broader vision of hyper-democracy.

6 Conclusion

Introducing an AI participant to online deliberation among Afghan youth meaningfully improved the quality, fluidity, and future-orientation of group dialogue. The AI's presence neither suppressed engagement nor imposed convergence. Further research should explore AI's role across varied settings and tasks, refining approaches for maximum social benefit.

Acknowledgments. This work was supported by JST CREST Grant Number JPMJCR20D1, Japan.

Disclosure of Interests. The authors have no competing interests to declare that are relevant to the content of this article.

References

1. Fukumura, K., Ito, T.: Can llm-powered multi-agent systems augment human creativity? evidence from brainstorming tasks, CI '25, pp. 20–29. Association for Computing Machinery, New York, NY, USA (2025). https://doi.org/10.1145/3715928.3737479
2. Gimpel, H., Lahmer, S., Wohl, M., Graf-Drasch, V.: Digital facilitation of group work to gain predictable performance. Group Decis. Negot. **33**(1), 113–145 (2024). https://doi.org/10.1007/s10726-023-09856-8
3. Hadfi, R., Okuhara, S., Haqbeen, J., Sahab, S., Ohnuma, S., Ito, T.: Conversational agents enhance women's contribution in online debates. Sci. Rep. **13**(1), 14534 (2023). https://doi.org/10.1038/s41598-023-41703-3
4. Haqbeen, J., Ito, T., Sahab, S.: AI-based mediation improves opinion solicitation in a large-scale online discussion: Experimental evidence from Kabul municipality. In: Proceedings of the IJCAI-PRICAI 2020 Workshop on AI for Social Good (2021)
5. Haqbeen, J., Sahab, S., Ito, T.: In solidarity with Ukraine through conversational ai via facebook ads: a case study of online discussion in 15 countries. In: Proceedings of the 24th Annual International Conference on Digital Government Research, DGO '23, pp. 639–641. Association for Computing Machinery, New York, NY, USA (2023). https://doi.org/10.1145/3598469.3598541
6. Haqbeen, J., Sahab, S., Ito, T.: Comparison of best paper award selection between program committee members and attendees: case of an international conference. In: 2024 IEEE/ACIS 9th International Conference on Big Data, Cloud Computing, and Data Science (BCD). pp. 65–72 (2024). https://doi.org/10.1109/BCD61269.2024.10743083
7. Haqbeen, J., Sahab, S., Ito, T., Rizzi, P.: Using decision support system to enable crowd identify neighborhood issues and its solutions for policy makers: an online experiment at Kabul municipal level. Sustainability **13**(21), 12069 (2021). https://doi.org/10.3390/su132112069
8. Haqbeen, J.A., Sahab, S., Ito, T.: Assessment of the LLM-based chatbots on student engagement and learning outcomes in Afghanistan. In: Conference on Digital Government Research, 26 (2025). https://doi.org/10.59490/dgo.2025.956, https://proceedings.open.tudelft.nl/DGO2025/article/view/956
9. Ito, T.: Discussion and negotiation support for crowd-scale consensus. In: Kilgour, D.M., Eden, C. (eds.) Handbook of Group Decision and Negotiation. Springer (2021). https://doi.org/10.1007/978-3-030-49629-6_41
10. Ito, T., Dong, Y., Haqbeen, J., Sahab, S., Matsuo, T.: Multiple ai agents that support crowd discussion (extended abstract). In: ACM Collective Intelligence 2024 (2024)
11. Ito, T., Hadfi, R., Suzuki, S.: An agent that facilitates crowd discussion. Group Decision and Negotiation pp. 1–27 (2021)
12. Ito, T., et al.: Agent-based crowd discussion support system and its societal experiments. In: Demazeau, Y., Holvoet, T., Corchado, J.M., Costantini, S. (eds.) PAAMS 2020. LNCS (LNAI), vol. 12092, pp. 430–433. Springer, Cham (2020). https://doi.org/10.1007/978-3-030-49778-1_41

13. Ito, T., Suzuki, S., Yamaguchi, N., Nishida, T., Hiraishi, K., Yoshino, K.: D-agree: crowd discussion support system based on automated facilitation agent. In: 35th AAAI Conference, Demonstration (2020)
14. Nass, C., Steuer, J., Tauber, E.R.: Computers are social actors. In: Proceedings of the SIGCHI Conference on Human Factors in Computing Systems, CHI '94, pp. 72–78. Association for Computing Machinery, New York, NY, USA (1994). https://doi.org/10.1145/191666.191703
15. Nomura, M., Ito, T., Ding, S.: Towards collaborative brain-storming among humans and ai agents: an implementation of the ibis-based brainstorming support system with multiple ai agents. In: Proceedings of the ACM Collective Intelligence Conference, CI '24, pp. 1–9. Association for Computing Machinery, New York, NY, USA (2024). https://doi.org/10.1145/3643562.3672609
16. Sahab, S., Haqbeen, J., Ito, T.: Facilitating the problems that lie within the solutions using conversational AI: a case study of post-2021 Afghanistan. In: Proceedings of the 24th Annual International Conference on Digital Government Research, DGO '23, pp. 654–656. Association for Computing Machinery, New York, NY, USA (2023). https://doi.org/10.1145/3598469.3598547
17. Sahab, S., Haqbeen, J., Ito, T.: Conversational ai as a facilitator improves participant engagement and problem-solving in online discussion: sharing evidence from five cities in Afghanistan. In: IEICE Transactions on Information and Systems pp. 1–10 (2024)
18. Tessler, M.H., Bakker, M.: AI can help humans find common ground in democratic deliberation. Science (2024)

Multi-Agent Learning

Large Batch Sharing

Thibault Lahire(✉)

Dassault Aviation, Saint-Cloud, France
thibault.lahire@dassault-aviation.com

Abstract. By reusing experiences collected from past different policies, experience replay significantly improves the training efficiency of reinforcement learning algorithms. Rapid convergence occurs when learning is based on pertinent experiences that offer valuable information. Nonetheless, how to effectively combine experience replay with multi-agent reinforcement learning is still an open challenge. We study how sharing collected experiences helps the training process and show that sharing a small amount of selected experiences between agents improves the learning process compared to the baseline where each agent is independent. The shared experiences are selected by each agent on internal statistics, ensuring their meaningfulness. Our first results on the multi-agent Pursuit environment highlight an improvement by a large margin and need to be consolidated by complementary experiences.

Keywords: Multi-Agent Deep Reinforcement Learning · Importance Sampling · Replay Buffers

1 Introduction

Multi-Agent Systems [15] have benefited from Reinforcement Learning [30, RL] as it enabled to address many issues [36]. In particular, RL has made improvements in adaptive decision-making [3], handles partial observability [25], promotes emergent behavior and self-organization [17], provides decentralized control tools [26] and allows agents to generalize over different tasks thanks to transfer learning [8]. However, when each agent learns independently, Multi-Agent Reinforcement Learning (MARL) experiences difficulties in the learning process due to the non-stationarity of the environment. Even though the convergence guarantees of MARL are an active field of research [13], MARL still succeeds in learning in complex environments [31].

In deep RL, neural network policies and value functions can be learnt thanks to stochastic gradient descent algorithms [27, SGD] sampling an experience replay memory [19]. This replay memory, or replay buffer, stores the transitions encountered along the interaction with the environment. SGD-based algorithms exploit such buffers to learn relevant functions, such as the Q-function in the case of Deep Q-Networks [22], the return distribution for distributional approaches [2], or an actor and a critic [11,18] in the case of continuous state-action space

J. Haqbeen et al. (Eds.): IJCAI 2025, LNAI 16400, pp. 73–83, 2026.
https://doi.org/10.1007/978-981-95-9667-6_6

problems. Most deep RL algorithms boildown to a sequence of SGD-based, supervised learning problems. In supervised learning, importance sampling can be used to speed up the convergence of SGD, by sampling non-uniformly the training set to reduce the variance of the stochastic gradient estimate. As there is a link between supervised learning and RL, accelerating the convergence thanks to non-uniform sampling has also been explored in the latter with Prioritized Experience Replay [28, PER], drawing inspiration from Prioritized Sweeping [23]. Extensions, modifications, and foundations of PER have been proposed, such as [16,34]. In this paper, we show that some of the techniques initially designed to accelerate convergence speed in the single-agent case can be used to help agents in their learning process.

In a partially observable environment which is "anonymous" (the environment behaves the same way for all agents) to homogeneous agents collecting at each time step their own reward, this work proposes a sharing-experience scheme among agents. Each agent is initialized with its own neural network and replay buffer. At each learning step, each agent updates its neural network parameters thanks to an SGD step with a mini-batch composed of experiences from its own replay buffer, as well as experiences collected by other agents. The relevance of a given experience to a given agent is checked before being used for the SGD step thanks to statistics specific to the updated agent. Our experience-sharing method compares to independent learning, where agents are initialized with their own neural network and replay buffer and do not share anything. We evaluate the benefit of sharing a small amount of experiences collected by other agents in a mixed collaborative-competitive environment.

This work is structured as follows. Section 2 covers related work in MARL and importance sampling for RL. Then Sect. 3 proposes an algorithm to improve learning in multi-agent settings by sampling efficiently useful experiences collected by the other agents. Section 4 empirically evaluates the proposed algorithm. We discuss each separate aspect of sampling, its explanations and perspectives. Section 5 discusses the limitations of this work and contrasts our findings with the existing literature. Section 6 summarizes and concludes.

2 Background

We model our MARL problem as a Partially Observable Stochastic Game (POSG), a generalization of Stochastic (Markov) Games [20] to settings where agents are only able to observe parts of the state of the environment [12]. A POSG is a tuple $(M, \mathcal{S}, \mathcal{A}, \mathcal{T}, \mathcal{R}, \mathcal{O}, \mathcal{T}_e)$, where M is the number of agents, $\mathcal{S}$ is the set of all possible global states of the environment, $\mathcal{A} := A_1 \times A_2 \times ... \times A_M$ represents the set of actions, where A_i is the action space of agent i, $\mathcal{T} : \mathcal{S} \times \mathcal{A} \rightarrow \Delta(\mathcal{S})$ is the transition probability function between global states, based on the joint action of the agents, $\mathcal{R} := R_1 \times R_2 \times ... \times R_M$ is the reward function, where $R_i : \mathcal{S} \times \mathcal{A} \times \mathcal{S} \rightarrow \mathbb{R}$ is the individual reward function of agent i, $\mathcal{O} := O_1 \times O_2 \times ... \times O_M$ is the set of observations with O_i representing the individual observation set for each agent i, and $\mathcal{T}_e : \mathcal{S} \times \mathcal{A} \rightarrow \Delta(\mathcal{O})$ is the observation function.

The behaviour of an agent is defined by its policy $\pi_i : O_i \times A_i \rightarrow [0, 1]$. The performance of a policy can be assessed through its Q-function $Q^{\pi_i} = \mathbb{E}[\sum_t \gamma^t r_{i,t} | \boldsymbol{\pi}]$, where $\boldsymbol{\pi} = (\pi_1, ..., \pi_M)$ is the joint policy of the agents acting in the environment, $\gamma \in [0, 1]$ is the discount factor, and $r_{i,t} = R_i(s_t, \boldsymbol{a}_t, s_{t+1})$ is the reward obtained by agent i at time step t for the joint action $\boldsymbol{a}_t \in \mathcal{A}$ at state $s_t \in \mathcal{S}$ and transitioning to the next state $s_{t+1} \in \mathcal{S}$. The goal of each agent is to find their policy π_i^* that has the largest possible Q-function.

As set previously, this work focuses on agents receiving their own reward in a partially observable environment that reacts to each agent the same way. If an action taken by an agent in a particular state yields reward, so does the environment for any other agent (the environment is said to be "anonymous"). We also make the assumption of homogeneous agents, sharing the same set of individual actions. All assumptions related to our multi-agent setting will be discussed in Sect. 5 along with extensions and limitations of our work.

In such a framework, two baseline algorithms can be used. First, one single agent, taking as input the observation and outputting the action for the agent receiving the observation can be trained thanks to the gathering of the agents' interactions with the environment. This method belongs to the Parameter Sharing (PS) algorithms, where neural network(s) and replay buffer (if any) are shared among all agents. The second baseline we consider are independent learners, where each agent trains its own neural network(s) thanks to its own interactions with the environment. Neural network(s) parameters (and replay buffers) remain private.

Our contribution, consisting in designing an efficient sharing of experiences between agents, can be applied to any underlying model-free deep RL algorithm using a replay buffer. For pedagogical purposes, we focus on the Deep Q-Networks [22, DQN] algorithm, which is off-policy and designed for discrete actions, and we will explain in Sect. 5 how the proposed methods can be extended to other settings.

In single-agent RL with full observability, the optimal Q-function obeys equation $Q^*(s, a) = \mathbb{E}_{s',r}[r + \gamma \max_{a'} Q^*(s', a')]$, called the Bellman optimality equation. DQN is the approximate Value Iteration algorithm that uses a replay buffer of N samples (s, a, r, s'), a deep neural network Q_θ, and a few steps of gradient descent to minimize the Bellman optimality equation. Specifically, at each training step, DQN aims to take a gradient step on the empirical loss $\frac{1}{N} \sum_{i=1}^{N} \ell(Q_\theta(s_i, a_i), y_i)$, with $y_i = r_i + \gamma \max_{a'} Q_n(s'_i, a')$. Minimization of this empirical loss by SGD implies drawing at each step a mini-batch of B transitions from the replay buffer and taking a descent step $\theta_{t+1} = \theta_t - \eta d$ in the direction of the gradient estimate $d = \frac{1}{B} \sum_{i=1}^{B} \nabla_\theta \ell(Q_\theta(s_i, a_i), y_i)$, with learning rate η.

To the best of our knowledge, Prioritized Experience Replay [28, PER] is the first work introducing a non-uniform sampling of the replay buffer to accelerate the convergence of the DQN algorithm from an empirical perspective. At each iteration, PER samples a mini-batch according to the probability distribution induced by a list of priorities, performs a gradient step and updates the

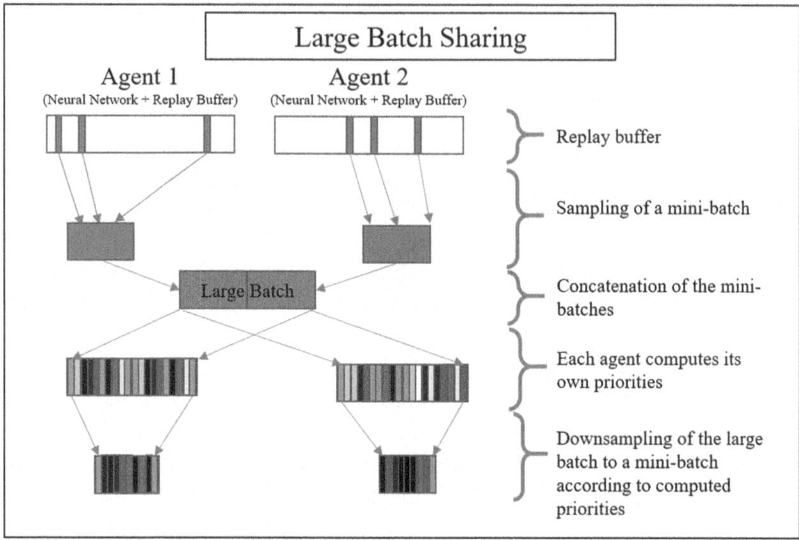

Fig. 1. Illustration of the Large Batch Sharing algorithm in the case of two agents.

priorities of the selected samples. PER drew inspiration from Prioritized Sweeping [23] and used TD errors as priorities without mathematical justification. Even though PER lacks theoretical foundations, a large number of publications experimentally demonstrate its benefits. Notably, the ablation study of [14] showed PER to be one of the most critical improvements over DQN. [16] cast prioritization of samples in RL as importance sampling and proposed non-uniform sampling schemes aiming at accelerating the convergence speed of SGD. It brought theoretical foundations to many prioritization algorithms, especially PER, and proposed more grounded sampling schemes. One of the proposed algorithm, LaBER (for Large Batch Experience Replay), consists in sampling uniformly a large batch from the replay buffer (hence the name), computing TD errors on this large batch and finally down-sampling the large batch to a mini-batch according to the distribution induced by the TD errors. Note that, contrarily to PER, the TD errors are up-to-date, and this difference allows a more accurate sampling scheme.

3 Large Batch Sharing

In this work, we reuse the idea of a large batch, but we fill it with experiences collected by all agents which communicate. Then, we compute the TD errors on this large batch and we down-sample the large batch to a mini-batch thanks to the distribution induced by the TD errors. Let B be the mini-batch size, and N be the size of the replay buffers. Let K be the large batch size, so that $K = BM$, where M is the number of agents. Our algorithm, named Large Batch Sharing and illustrated in Fig. 1, goes as follows.

For each agent $i \in [1; M]$, 1/ draw a mini-batch of size B from the replay buffer with distribution p_1. Aggregate the $M-1$ other mini-batches to obtain the large batch. 2/ On this large batch, compute probability distribution p_2 and down-sample the large batch to a mini-batch thanks to this distribution. 3/ Finally, perform the SGD step thanks to the samples in the mini-batch. We now detail the subtleties at each step previously described.

Step 1 of the algorithm could simply consist in drawing uniformly a mini-batch from the replay buffer (hence $p_1 = u$, where $u_i = 1/N$, $\forall i \in [1; N]$), but we will test different sampling, such as PER.

Step 2 computes the priority which determines which samples will yield the better SGD step thanks to distribution p_2. Note that, if p_2 and p_1 are both uniform distributions, then our algorithm is strictly equivalent to a parameter sharing baseline where replay buffers are fully shared, but neural networks are not. We will, of course, test this baseline but our aim is to explore different sampling schemes. In particular, as proposed in LaBER, we take p_2 as the distribution induced by the TD-errors. By doing this, we ensure that the samples coming from other agents really help in taking better SGD steps.

Step 3 must be carefully implemented. As explained previously, the SGD step in its standard form for the DQN algorithm, sampling uniformly a replay buffer with a mini-batch of size B is

$$\theta_{t+1} = \theta_t - \eta \frac{1}{B} \sum_{i=1}^{B} \nabla_\theta l_i(\theta) \tag{1}$$

with $l_i(\theta) = (r_i + \gamma \max_{a'_i} Q_{\bar{\theta}}(s'_i, a'_i) - Q_\theta(s_i, a_i))^2$. When importance sampling is used to obtain the mini-batch, the update equation depends on the probability distribution q (over the N items of the replay buffer) used for sampling (see [16] for more details):

$$\theta_{t+1} = \theta_t - \eta \frac{1}{B} \sum_{i=1}^{B} \frac{1}{N q_i} \nabla_\theta l_i(\theta). \tag{2}$$

From a theoretical point of view, we cannot discriminate between the two. Indeed, in our multi-agent framework, the data distribution on which the learning is rooted is unknown, contrarily to supervised learning. The distribution of collected experiences from which agents can learn optimally their tasks remains unknown. Hence we cannot assess the quality of an update equation in our multi-agent RL case using importance sampling. We will test different update equations.

4 Experiments

Even though many experiences remain to be run, the first results obtain on the SISL (Stanford Intelligent Systems Laboratory) environment named Pursuit appear promising [10]. In the Pursuit scenario, a mixed collaborative-competitive environment is presented, involving a team of pursuers aiming to capture a

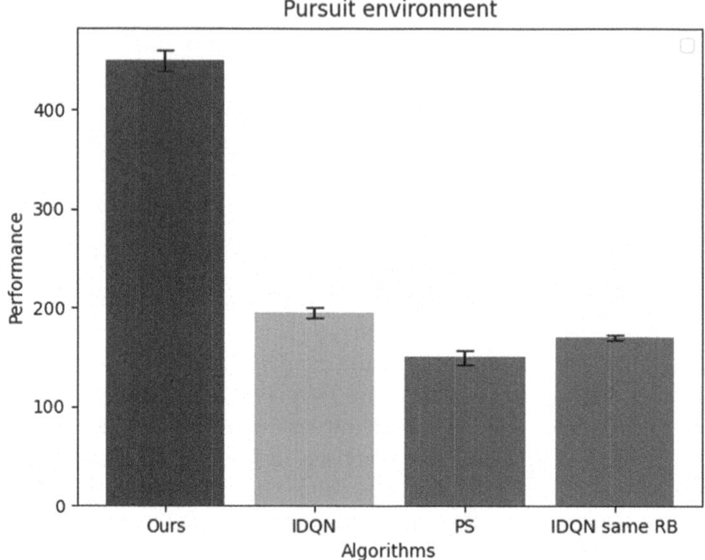

Fig. 2. Performance of the four agents in Pursuit at 800k timesteps.

group of evaders within a grid-world containing obstacles. The evaders, depicted in blue, move randomly, while the pursuers, represented in red, are under the control of RL agents. When a group of two or more agents successfully surrounds an evader, each agent receives a reward, and the evader is eliminated from the environment. The episode concludes either when all evaders are captured or after 500 steps, whichever comes first. Pursuers earn a small reward for being adjacent to an evader (even without complete surrounding) and incur a slight negative reward per timestep, encouraging them to complete episodes promptly. The setup involves 8 pursuers and 30 evaders. We perform the training for 800k timesteps and average our results over 10 seeds (Fig. 2).

As explained earlier, the two baselines are 1/ the independent DQN agents (IDQN), and 2/ the parameter sharing agent (PS) owning one neural network and replay buffer collecting all experiments. Our agent uses p_1 as the uniform distribution, and p_2 as the distribution induced by the up-to-date TD errors. We use Eq. 1 for the SGD update. The fourth algorithm tested (IDQN same RB) consists in taking p_1 and p_2 as the uniform distribution. In this case, each agent has its own neural network but the replay buffer is shared by all agents. All hyperparameters for the DQN base agent are the same for all the tested configurations to ensure a fair comparison and are reported in Table 1.

Figure 1 shows the average sum of rewards per episode at the end of training for each tested algorithm. This result advocates for a high benefit of our sampling but remains to be consolidated by other experiments. In particular, a sensitivity analysis with respect to hyper-parameters specific to our method have to be tested. We plan to analyze the impact of: 1/ the amount of experiences to share

Table 1. Hyperparameters

Environment hyperparamters	Value
max cycles	500
shared reward	False
horizon	500
surrounded	True
tag reward	0.01
constrained window	1.0
obs range	7
x/y sizes	16/16
num evaders	30
n catch	2
n agents (pursuers)	8
urgency reward	−0.1
catch rewards	5
CNN network hyperparameters	Value
CNN layers	[32, 64, 64]
Stride	1
Kernel size	[2, 2]
DQN hyperparameters	Value
learning rate	0.00016
mini-batch size	32
buffer size	120000
initial exploration epsilon	0.1
final exploration epsilon	0.001
target network update freq	1000
factor K	8

between agents, 2/ the sampling distribution used for p_1 and p_2, and 3/ the update equation for SGD (either Eq. 1 or Eq. 2).

5 Discussions, Limitations and Related Work

Our work restricts to homogeneous agents. An experience can be useful to another agent only if this agent can also take the action of the experience. Moreover, in the case of heterogeneous agents, where agents do not share the same action space, the baseline algorithms are different. In particular, the parameter sharing baseline is not applicable. Our work also restricts to "anonymous" environments and could not be extended to a different setting, where a certain action combined with a certain observation does not yield the same reward to all agents.

Note that this kind of environment is rare in practice, and when encountered, it is often in the case of heterogeneous agents, as in [4].

Our contribution is illustrated on collaborative systems, and it also applies to mixed and competitive settings, as long as agents remain homogeneous and the environment anonymous. We found more intuitive to highlight the benefits of sharing experiences on collaborative settings, as parameter sharing is rarely seen in practice on competitive environments. Indeed, in such settings, agents often explore the environment for their own profit, avoiding sharing information to maintain an advantage in the environment knowledge compared to the competitors.

In cooperative multi-agent systems, where all agents share the same reward at each step, our contribution can be used as well. However, note that cooperative tasks are harder to solve compared to collaborative ones, where each agent earns its own reward, due to the credit assignment problem. Even though it remains to be experimentally verified, we suspect our method to be less beneficial in this setting. Sharing experiments between agents is likely to make the credit assignment even more harder to solve, since knowing property of one experiment might help the credit assignment.

This work focuses on the DQN algorithm, as it is a common practice in the single-agent literature to study importance sampling and prioritization on this base agent. Our contribution extends directly to all off-policy algorithms using a replay buffer to learn a value function. This encompasses algorithms designed for continuous actions, such as DDPG [18], TD3 [9], SAC [11], and also distributional RL agents, such as C51 [2], QR-DQN [6], and IQN [5]. Sharing experiences can also be performed with on-policy algorithms such as PPO [29]. However, as prioritizing samples with policy-based algorithms remains a difficult problem, even in the single-agent setting, we keep this extension of our algorithm for future works.

This enumeration of limitations is necessary to understand the scope of our study and to place it in the literature. Perhaps the most similar work to ours is [35]. The authors use PER to select the shared experiences, but do not check the relevance of a particular sample for the agent which receives it, which is what we propose in our work. [7] couple multi-task RL algorithms with a task-sampling policy based on the intrinsic motivation paradigm. [24] propose an exploration strategy which enables to fill the replay buffer with experiences collected from a distribution supposed to be beneficial for the learning process.

Prioritized sampling has also been studied in multi-agent RL in settings different to ours. In cooperative tasks, an extended literature has been produced in recent years studying the interplay between non-stationarity, credit assignment, and importance sampling. For instance, [21] derives an importance sampling scheme allowing to correct the distribution of the replay buffers, hence enabling a better convergence. [1] compare to [21] but frame their study in model-based MARL. [32] study how PER can improve offline MARL thanks to a trajectory selection using Graph Attention Networks [33].

6 Conclusion

This work focuses on an efficient experience sharing scheme between homogeneous agents learning in an anonymous environment. This scheme draws inspiration from the optimization literature, and our work remains an empirical study as no convergence or improvement guarantees can be derived. This article remains a work in progress, and the first experimental results highlight the benefit of sharing a small amount of experiences between agents.

In the near future, complementary experiments have to be run. Different environments have to be tested, as well as different numbers of agents. In particular, we would like to confirm/infirm the following intuition: Our method brings a significant improvement on tasks where the independent learners baseline performs well, in environments necessitating specialization of agents. Complementary experiments will also study from an empirical point of view the amount of experiments to be shared between agents yielding the best learning improvement.

References

1. Bargiacchi, E., Verstraeten, T., Roijers, D.M., Nowé, A.: Model-based multi-agent reinforcement learning with cooperative prioritized sweeping. arXiv preprint arXiv:2001.07527 (2020)
2. Bellemare, M.G., Dabney, W., Munos, R.: A distributional perspective on reinforcement learning. In: International Conference on Machine Learning, pp. 449–458. PMLR (2017)
3. Busoniu, L., Babuska, R., De Schutter, B.: A comprehensive survey of multiagent reinforcement learning. IEEE Trans. Syst. Man Cybern. Part C (Applications and Reviews) **38**(2), 156–172 (2008)
4. Calvo, J.A., Dusparic, I.: Heterogeneous multi-agent deep reinforcement learning for traffic lights control. In: AICS, pp. 2–13 (2018)
5. Dabney, W., Ostrovski, G., Silver, D., Munos, R.: Implicit quantile networks for distributional reinforcement learning. In: International Conference on Machine Learning, pp. 1096–1105. PMLR (2018)
6. Dabney, W., Rowland, M., Bellemare, M., Munos, R.: Distributional reinforcement learning with quantile regression. In: Proceedings of the AAAI Conference on Artificial Intelligence, vol. 32 (2018)
7. D'Eramo, C., Chalvatzaki, G.: Prioritized sampling with intrinsic motivation in multi-task reinforcement learning. In: 2022 International Joint Conference on Neural Networks (IJCNN), pp. 1–8. IEEE (2022)
8. Foerster, J., Assael, I.A., De Freitas, N., Whiteson, S.: Learning to communicate with deep multi-agent reinforcement learning. Adv. Neural Inf. Process. Syst. **29** (2016)
9. Fujimoto, S., Hoof, H., Meger, D.: Addressing function approximation error in actor-critic methods. In: International Conference on Machine Learning, pp. 1587–1596 (2018)
10. Gupta, J.K., Egorov, M., Kochenderfer, M.: Cooperative multi-agent control using deep reinforcement learning. In: Autonomous Agents and Multiagent Systems: AAMAS 2017 Workshops, Best Papers, São Paulo, Brazil, May 8-12, 2017, Revised Selected Papers 16, pp. 66–83. Springer (2017)

11. Haarnoja, T., Zhou, A., Abbeel, P., Levine, S.: Soft actor-critic: off-policy maximum entropy deep reinforcement learning with a stochastic actor. In: International Conference on Machine Learning, pp. 1861–1870 (2018)
12. Hansen, E.A., Bernstein, D.S., Zilberstein, S.: Dynamic programming for partially observable stochastic games. In: Proceedings of the 19th National Conference on Artifical Intelligence, pp. 709–715 (2004)
13. Hernandez-Leal, P., Kartal, B., Taylor, M.E.: A survey and critique of multiagent deep reinforcement learning. Auton. Agent. Multi-Agent Syst. **33**(6), 750–797 (2019)
14. Hessel, M., et al.: Rainbow: combining improvements in deep reinforcement learning. In: Thirty-Second AAAI Conference on Artificial Intelligence (2018)
15. Van der Hoek, W., Wooldridge, M.: Multi-agent systems. Found. Artif. Intell. **3**, 887–928 (2008)
16. Lahire, T., Geist, M., Rachelson, E.: Large batch experience replay. In: International Conference on Machine Learning, pp. 11790–11813. PMLR (2022)
17. Li, Z., Sim, C.H., Low, M.Y.H.: A survey of emergent behavior and its impacts in agent-based systems. In: 2006 4th IEEE International Conference on Industrial Informatics, pp. 1295–1300. IEEE (2006)
18. Lillicrap, T.P., et al.: Continuous control with deep reinforcement learning. In: ICLR (Poster) (2016)
19. Lin, L.J.: Self-improving reactive agents based on reinforcement learning, planning and teaching. Mach. Learn. **8**(3–4), 293–321 (1992)
20. Littman, M.L.: Markov games as a framework for multi-agent reinforcement learning. In: Machine Learning Proceedings 1994, pp. 157–163. Elsevier (1994)
21. Mei, Y., Zhou, H., Lan, T., Venkataramani, G., Wei, P.: MAC-PO: Multi-agent experience replay via collective priority optimization. arXiv preprint arXiv:2302.10418 (2023)
22. Mnih, V., et al.: Human-level control through deep reinforcement learning. Nature **518**(7540), 529–533 (2015)
23. Moore, A.W., Atkeson, C.G.: Prioritized sweeping: reinforcement learning with less data and less time. Mach. Learn. **13**(1), 103–130 (1993)
24. Nicholaus, I.T., Kang, D.K.: Robust experience replay sampling for multi-agent reinforcement learning. Pattern Recogn. Lett. **155**, 135–142 (2022)
25. Omidshafiei, S., Pazis, J., Amato, C., How, J.P., Vian, J.: Deep decentralized multi-task multi-agent reinforcement learning under partial observability. In: International Conference on Machine Learning, pp. 2681–2690. PMLR (2017)
26. Panait, L., Luke, S.: Cooperative multi-agent learning: the state of the art. Auton. Agent. Multi-Agent Syst. **11**, 387–434 (2005)
27. Robbins, H., Monro, S.: A stochastic approximation method. Ann. Math. Stat. 400–407 (1951)
28. Schaul, T., Quan, J., Antonoglou, I., Silver, D.: Prioritized experience replay. In: ICLR (Poster) (2016)
29. Schulman, J., Wolski, F., Dhariwal, P., Radford, A., Klimov, O.: Proximal policy optimization algorithms. arXiv preprint arXiv:1707.06347 (2017)
30. Sutton, R.S., Barto, A.G.: Reinforcement Learning: An Introduction. MIT Press (2018)
31. Tampuu, A., et al.: Multiagent cooperation and competition with deep reinforcement learning. PLoS ONE **12**(4), e0172395 (2017)
32. Tian, Q., Kuang, K., Liu, F., Wang, B.: Learning from good trajectories in offline multi-agent reinforcement learning. In: Proceedings of the AAAI Conference on Artificial Intelligence. vol. 37, pp. 11672–11680 (2023)

33. Veličković, P., Cucurull, G., Casanova, A., Romero, A., Liò, P., Bengio, Y.: Graph attention networks. In: International Conference on Learning Representations (2018)
34. Wang, C., Ross, K.: Boosting soft actor-critic: Emphasizing recent experience without forgetting the past. arXiv preprint arXiv:1906.04009 (2019)
35. Wang, Y., Zhang, Z.: Experience selection in multi-agent deep reinforcement learning. In: 2019 IEEE 31st International Conference on Tools with Artificial Intelligence (ICTAI), pp. 864–870. IEEE (2019)
36. Zhang, K., Yang, Z., Başar, T.: Multi-agent reinforcement learning: a selective overview of theories and algorithms. Handbook of Reinforcement Learning and Control, pp. 321–384 (2021)

Diversified Experience Replay for Multi-agent Reinforcement Learning

Guangchong Zhou[1,2], Feng Hong[3], Zeren Zhang[1,2], and Guoliang Fan[1](✉)

[1] The Key Laboratory of Cognition and Decision Intelligence for Complex Systems, Institute of Automation, Chinese Academy of Sciences, Beijing, China
{zhouguangchong2021,zhangzeren2021,guoliang.fan}@ia.ac.cn

[2] School of Artificial Intelligence, University of Chinese Academy of Sciences, Beijing, China

[3] Cooperative Medianet Innovation Center, Shanghai Jiao Tong University, Shanghai, China
feng.hong@sjtu.edu.cn

Abstract. To enhance the capability of off-policy multi-agent reinforcement learning (MARL), previous research has extensively investigated the agents' decision-making and credit assignment. However, the role of experience replay is largely overlooked, with related works limited to prioritizing samples based on their TD-errors. Despite their improvements, more accurate Q-value estimations do not guarantee better decisions, as the relative advantage of different situations is more crucial for the greedy policy. To this end, we propose **Div**ersified **E**xperience **R**eplay (DivER), which increases the experience diversity in the sampled mini-batch. Agents are guided to learn behaviors that transition to more superior situations, thus enhancing training efficiency. DivER is compatible with any off-policy MARL methods and has been experimentally proven to be effective across various tasks and algorithms.

Keywords: Off-policy MARL · Prioritized experience replay · Sample diversity

1 Introduction

Multi-Agent Reinforcement Learning (MARL) has emerged as a powerful paradigm for tackling complex sequential decision-making problems involving multiple interacting agents, with applications spanning flocking control [7,41], autonomous driving [30,45], and traffic light control [40]. A critical factor in the practical success of MARL algorithms is *sample efficiency*, due to costly agent interactions. Off-policy methods [26,34], by enabling agents to learn from past experiences, offer a promising avenue for enhanced data utilization, typically through an experience replay buffer.

To improve experience replay for MARL upon naive uniform sampling strategy, a predominant approach is the direct adaptation of Prioritized Experience Replay (PER) [28] and its variants from single-agent reinforcement learning. PER-based methods typically prioritize the samples with high magnitude of TD-errors to improve global Q-value estimations, under the premise that the task

J. Haqbeen et al. (Eds.): IJCAI 2025, LNAI 16400, pp. 84–104, 2026.
https://doi.org/10.1007/978-981-95-9667-6_7

is fully learnable without stochasticity in rewards or transitions. While these adaptations have shown utility, they do not explicitly account for the unique multi-agent dynamics, such as partial observability and individual-global policy monotonicity [26]. To our knowledge, MAC-PO [18] is the only work to date that specifically redesigns for multi-agent setting, which prioritizes the samples in replay buffer via regret minimization. However, due to the frequent concentration of samples with large errors or regret values in specific regions of the entire space, these methods often lead to a loss of sample diversity.

Figure 1 shows the results of different mini-batch sampling strategies on a toy replay buffer. It can be seen that the default uniform sampling strategy does not guarantee comprehensive coverage of all experiences, while the outcomes of PER based on TD-error exhibit significant homogeneity and imbalance. We argue that, as agents in most off-policy methods are value-based and employ greedy policies, the relative superiority among different states can better guide the agents' decision-making towards superior states rather than precise state value estimations. Therefore, at each training step, a mini-batch with greater sample diversity is more conducive to the agent's understanding of the relative merits of different experiences, thereby accelerating policy improvement. To this end, we propose **Div**ersified **E**xperience **R**eplay (DivER), a novel and flexible method to improve the sample diversity of the mini-batch at each training step. To accommodate the partial observability of multi-agent tasks, DivER learns a representation model to transform the entire episode of states into a compact vector, based on which it measures the discrepancy between experiences in the replay buffer and generates a mini-batch of diversified samples. Our main contributions can be summarized as follows:

- **A New Perspective**: We explore the multi-agent experience replay, which is largely overlooked by previous research, and are the very first to consider the sample diversity of the mini-batch, thereby furnishing a novel perspective for subsequent studies.
- **A New Approach**: We propose a prioritized experience replay method called DivER for enhanced sample diversity of the mini-batch at each training step. As DivER only modifies the experience replay mechanism without altering the MARL framework, it can serve as a plug-and-play technique for any off-policy MARL methods and achieve stable improvements.
- **Strong Empirical Results**: We integrate DivER with multiple popular off-policy MARL methods and conduct extensive experiments across various environments. Results consistently demonstrate the superiority of DivER in improving sample efficiency while maintaining the convergence performance of off-policy MARL methods.

2 Related Works

2.1 Off-Policy MARL

In off-policy multi-agent reinforcement learning (MARL), agents learn from past experiences collected using a policy different from the current one, thereby

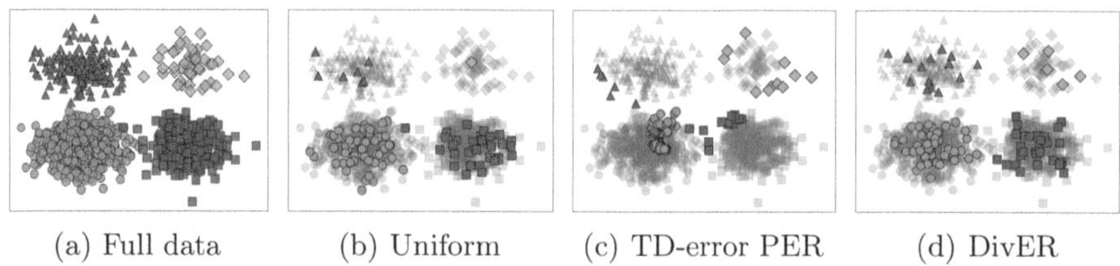

(a) Full data (b) Uniform (c) TD-error PER (d) DivER

Fig. 1. The comparison of different sampling methods on a toy replay buffer, in which the transition data is distributed in four regions. (a) The visualization of all data in the replay buffer. (b)(c)(d) The mini-batch derived by the Uniform, PER, and DivER sampling strategies.

improving the data efficiency. Value-based MARL algorithms are almost exclusively off-policy. Independent Q-learning [36] trains independent action-value functions for each agent, which is later combined with deep learning techniques by [35]. Under the CTDE framework, value decomposition is widely used to achieve credit assignment. VDN [34] and QMIX [26] estimate the optimal joint action-value function by combining mentioned utilities via a summation function and a learned state-dependent monotonic function, respectively. QTRAN [31] and QPLEX [37] further loose the monotonicity constraints in QMIX and extend the class of value functions. Weighted-QMIX [25] introduces a weighting mechanism into the projection of monotonic value factorization to place more importance on better joint actions. QPro [17] casts the factorization problem as regret minimization over the projection weights of different state-action values. For policy-based off-policy methods, MADDPG [16] utilizes the ensemble of policies for each agent that leads to more robust multi-agent policies, showing strength in cooperative and competitive scenarios. The extensions [6,9,32] of MADDPG have been proposed to realize further improvements on the original algorithm.

2.2 Experience Replay

Online reinforcement suffers from two issues: (a) strongly correlated transitions that break the i.i.d. assumption in deep learning, and (b) the rapid forgetting of possibly rare experiences that would be useful later on. Experience replay [13] stores the collected experiences in a replay buffer for subsequent reuse, which effectively mitigates the above issues and improves the sample efficiency. While most off-policy methods uniformly sample transitions from the replay buffer, [28] asserts that some experiences are more valuable for model training than others and proposes prioritized experience replay (PER), which replays transitions with higher magnitude of temporal-difference (TD) error more frequently. Subsequently, further modifications and improvements have been made to the PER algorithm. [12] design a sampling technique that updates the transitions backward from a whole episode. PSER [2] prioritizes sequences of experience instead of single transitions. ERO [44] learns a replay policy to optimize the prioritization function. To favor recent transitions and abandon the outdated ones,

[33] sample transitions according to the similarities between their states and the agent's state, while [19] control the similarity between the replay behaviors and the current policy. [14] use the regret minimization method to design the prioritized experience replay scheme. MaPER [20] improves experience replay by using a model-augmented critic network and modifying the rule of priority. So far, most PER works are designed for single-agent reinforcement learning. To extend PER to multi-agent scenarios, some research directly migrates previous works to off-policy MARL methods [4,39], while a limited number of studies consider the adaptation to multi-agent systems [1,18].

3 Background

3.1 Dec-POMDP

A fully cooperative multi-agent system (MAS) is typically represented by a decentralized partially observable Markov decision process (Dec-POMDP) [21], which is composed of a tuple $G = \langle \mathcal{S}, \boldsymbol{\mathcal{U}}, \mathcal{P}, \mathcal{Z}, r, \mathcal{O}, n, \gamma \rangle$. At each time-step, the current global state of the environment is denoted by $s \in \mathcal{S}$, while each agent $a \in \mathcal{A} := \{1, \dots, n\}$ only receives a unique local observation $z_a \in \mathcal{Z}$ generated by the observation function $\mathcal{O}(s, a) : \mathcal{S} \times \mathcal{A} \to \mathcal{Z}$. Subsequently, every agent a selects an action $u_a \in \mathcal{U}$, and all individual actions are combined to form the joint action $\boldsymbol{u} = [u_1, \dots, u_n] \in \boldsymbol{\mathcal{U}} \equiv \mathcal{U}^n$. The interaction between the joint action $\boldsymbol{u}$ and the current state s leads to a change in the environment to state s' as dictated by the state transition function $\mathcal{P}(s'|s, \boldsymbol{u}) : \mathcal{S} \times \mathcal{U} \times \mathcal{S} \to [0, 1]$. All agents in the Dec-POMDP share the same global reward function $r(s, \boldsymbol{u}) : \mathcal{S} \times \boldsymbol{\mathcal{U}} \to \mathbb{R}$, and $\gamma \in [0, 1)$ represents the discount factor.

3.2 One-Shot Coreset Selection

In supervised learning, let us consider a classification task with a training dataset containing N examples drawn i.i.d. from an underlying distribution P. The dataset is denoted as $\mathcal{D} = \{(\boldsymbol{x}_i, y_i)\}_{i=1}^{N}$, where $\boldsymbol{x}_i$ is the data and y_i is the ground-truth label. Given a pruning rate $\alpha \in (0, 1)$, the goal of one-shot coreset selection is to select a training subset $\mathcal{B}$ from the whole dataset to maximize the accuracy of models trained on this subset, which can be formulated as the optimization problem below [29]:

$$\min_{\mathcal{B} \subset \mathcal{D}, \frac{|\mathcal{B}|}{|\mathcal{D}|} \leq 1-\alpha} \mathbb{E}_{(\boldsymbol{x}, y) \sim P} \left[l \left(\boldsymbol{x}, y; h_{\mathcal{B}} \right) \right], \tag{1}$$

where $l(\cdot, \cdot)$ is the loss function, and $h_{\mathcal{B}}$ is the model trained on the subset $\mathcal{B}$. To find the optimal subset, previous methods typically rank the examples based on their importance and select the most important $|\mathcal{B}|$ examples to form the subset. Different metrics, including prediction error [10,15], gradient norm [11], area under the margin (AUM) [24], and EL2N score [23], are proposed to measure the importance of each sample.

Off-policy MARL methods commonly employ the replay buffer, from which a mini-batch of samples are selected for subsequent model updates. However, the training process of MARL differs significantly from supervised learning, and the design of effective coreset selection (known as prioritized experience replay) methods for MARL requires further investigation.

4 DivER

4.1 Motivation

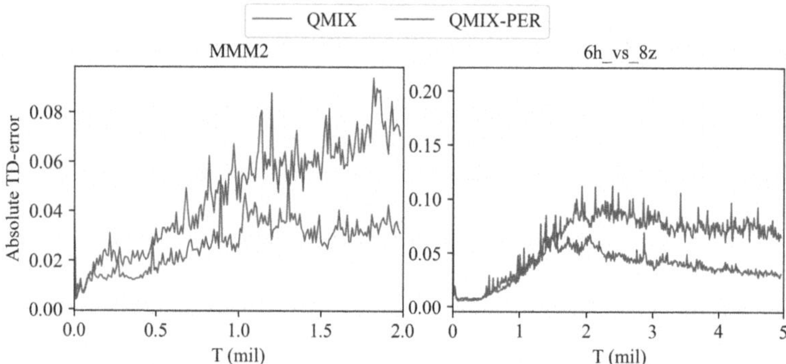

Fig. 2. The absolute value of TD-error during the training processes of QMIX with and w/o PER on two SMAC scenarios.

In this section, we mainly focus on value-based methods and use $\mathcal{D}$ and $\mathcal{B}$ to denote the replay buffer and sampled mini-batch in MARL, respectively. Most existing methods directly extend PER [28] to MARL, which prioritizes the samples with high magnitude of TD-errors. Therefore, these methods still follow the supervised learning target in Eq. 1 with the following loss function:

$$l(s_t, \boldsymbol{u}_t, r_t, s_{t+1}) = \left(r_t + \gamma \max_{\boldsymbol{u}_{t+1}} Q^-_{tot}(s_{t+1}, \boldsymbol{u}_{t+1}) - Q_{tot}(s_t, \boldsymbol{u}_t) \right)^2,$$

in which s_t and $\boldsymbol{u}_t$ are the global state and joint action at time step t, Q^-_{tot} is a periodically updated target network of Q_{tot}. As the experiment results in Fig. 2 show, the absolute value of TD-error during the training process of QMIX [26] is significantly reduced with the integration of PER (named QMIX-PER), indicating that PER effectively improves the accuracy of Q-value estimation. However, a more accurate value estimation does not necessarily lead to the policy improvement and the increase in the overall return of the system. Considering the training paradigm of MARL, we modify the objective for mini-batch selection at each training step to Eq. 2:

$$\begin{aligned}
&\max_{\mathcal{B}\subset\mathcal{D}} J(\pi') - J(\pi) \\
&= \max_{\mathcal{B}\subset\mathcal{D}} \mathbb{E}_{s_0}[V^{\pi'}(s_0)] - \mathbb{E}_{s_0}[V^{\pi}(s_0)] \\
&= \max_{\mathcal{B}\subset\mathcal{D}} \mathbb{E}_{\pi'}\left[\sum_{t=0}^{\infty} \gamma^t \left[r(s_t, a_t) + \gamma V^{\pi}(s_{t+1}) - V^{\pi}(s_t)\right]\right],
\end{aligned} \tag{2}$$

where π' is the updated policy based on π after trained on mini-batch $\mathcal{B}$ and $V(\cdot)$ is the state value function. We assert that, rather than precisely predicting the system value in every state, understanding the relative superiority among states could be more helpful in guiding the agents to learn behaviors that transition to superior states, thus facilitating efficient policy improvement. To this end, we propose **Div**ersified **E**xperience **R**eplay (DivER), which enhances the training efficiency by increasing the experience diversity in the sampled mini-batch.

4.2 Learning Episode Representation

Unlike single-agent tasks, each piece of data in MARL includes information from all time steps of an entire episode from start to end. Therefore, a single state at a specific time step cannot sufficiently represent the whole episode, nor can it be directly used to compare similarities with other episodes. Instead, we treat the sequence of states in an episode as a trajectory τ of the system, and summarize them into a compact vector z. The mutual information between τ and z measures the reduction of the uncertainty of trajectory prediction after knowing the representation z, which is defined as Eq. 3. By maximizing the mutual information, we extract the underlying latent information that the trajectory and its representation have in common.

$$\mathcal{I}(\tau; z) = \sum_{\tau, z} p(\tau, z) \log \frac{p(\tau|z)}{p(\tau)} \tag{3}$$

Next, it is necessary to design a learnable network architecture based on the training objectives. A severe challenge is that a powerful generative model for $p(\tau|z)$ in Eq. 3 is computationally intense and would waste capacity at modeling the complex relationships between the states in the sequence. Besides, unimodal losses like mean squared error and cross-entropy are not sufficient for predicting high-dimensional data. Inspired by [22], we do not predict the future trajectory directly with a generative model, but we model a density ratio which preserves the mutual information between the next trajectory τ_{t+1} and the representation of current trajectory z_t as:

$$f(x_{t+1}, z_t) \propto \frac{p(x_{t+1}|z_t)}{p(x_{t+1})}, \tag{4}$$

in which $\tau_{t+1} = [\tau_t, x_{t+1}]$ is simplified to x_{t+1}, since τ_t is already known when calculating z_t. To guarantee the output of f is a positive real score, we implement it with a simple log-bilinear function:

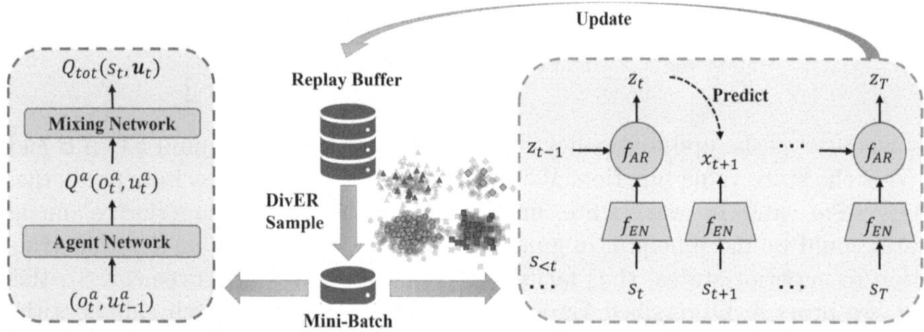

Fig. 3. Overview of DivER architecture. Red dashed box depicts the off-policy MARL method. Green dashed box is the representation model in DivER. f_{EN} and f_{AR} denote the state encoder and the autoregressive model respectively. (Color figure online)

$$f(x_{t+1}, z_t) = \exp\left(x_{t+1}^T W z_t\right), \tag{5}$$

where x_{t+1} is the encoded state at next step. More complex networks can also be used to construct f. With the density ratio as an alternative object, the networks are relieved from modeling the high dimensional trajectory. Though the distribution $p(\tau)$ or $p(\tau|z)$ cannot be evaluated by the model, we can estimate them using samples from the replay buffer instead. The overall architecture of DivER is depicted in Fig. 3, and it can be clearly seen that the workflow of DivER is fully decoupled from the MARL framework. At each time step, the state is encoded and fed into the autoregressive model to generate the trajectory representation z_t, which helps predict the encoded state x_{t+1} at next step.

Consider a mini-batch $\mathcal{B}$ of N episodes with length T. For each episode, z_t has one positive label $p(x_{t+1}^i|z_t)$ and $N-1$ negative samples $\{x_{t+1}^j|j = 1, ..., i-1, i+1, ..., N\}$ from other episodes. By referring to contrastive learning [8,22], we learn the representation model by maximizing the target in Eq. 6 as the following lemma holds:

Lemma 1. *Equation 6 is a lower bound for mutual information $\mathcal{I}(x_{t+1}, z_t)$, and maximizing it leads to $f(x_{t+1}, z_t)$ approximating the density ratio in Eq. 4.*

$$\mathcal{J}_D = \sum_{i=1}^{N} \sum_{t=1}^{T-1} \log \frac{f(x_{t+1}^i, z_t^i)}{\sum_{j=1}^{N} f(x_{t+1}^j, z_t^j)} \tag{6}$$

Proof. See Appendix A.1.

With the learned representation model, we can summarize the whole state sequence of length T into a compact vector z_T for downstream tasks.

4.3 Sampling Methodology

Next, we need to sample episodes from the replay buffer to obtain the mini-batch based on their trajectory representations. Previous methods for prioritized experience replay commonly measure the importance of samples using metrics such as training errors and gradients, then rank the samples and select the most significant ones. However, the ranking approach is not applicable to DivER, as "diversity" is not an attribute possessed by a single agent but rather a global metric for the overall system. Identifying a fixed-size mini-batch with the optimal diversity from the replay buffer constitutes an NP problem, making it both impractical and unworthy to solve. Therefore, the sampling strategy of DivER needs to strike a balance between diversity and computational efficiency. Given a replay buffer $\mathcal{D}$ and sampled mini-batch $\mathcal{B}$, we first employ the concept of "coverage radius" to interpret the diversity:

Definition 1 (r-cover and coverage radius). *A set of points $\mathcal{D}$ are distributed in a metric space (X, d). We say mini-batch $\mathcal{B} \subset \mathcal{D}$ is a r-cover of $\mathcal{D}$ if:*

$$\mathcal{D} \subseteq \bigcup_{x \in \mathcal{B}} B(x, r),$$

where $B(x, r) = \{x' \in X | d(x', x) < r\}$ is an open ball of radius r centered at point x. The lower bound of r is called the coverage radius.

When the mini-batch size is fixed, a smaller coverage radius indicates that the mini-batch encompasses diverse episodes and represents the entire replay buffer more sufficiently. While existing methods like uniform sampling and PER can not guarantee a small coverage radius due to randomness and distribution imbalance, we propose a new sampling methodology for DivER presented in Algorithm 1.

Simply speaking, we first cluster the trajectory representations z_T of different episodes in the latent space to obtain multiple spherical clusters. Next, DivER uniformly samples an equal proportion of episodes from each cluster, which are then merged to form the final mini-batch. The episodes from different clusters help maintain a low coverage radius and high sample diversity for the mini-batch $\mathcal{B}$, while the uniform sampling within each cluster guarantees the computational efficiency of DivER.

Algorithm 1. DivER Sampling

Inputs:
Replay buffer $\mathcal{D}$, mini-batch size N

Cluster samples in $\mathcal{D}$ based on z_T,
$\mathcal{D}' \leftarrow \{\mathbb{D}_i | \mathbb{D}_i$ contains samples from the i-th cluster$\}$,
$\mathcal{B} \leftarrow \emptyset$.
while $\mathcal{D}' \neq \emptyset$ **do**
    $\mathbb{D}_{\min} \leftarrow \arg\min_{\mathbb{D}_i \in \mathcal{D}'} |\mathbb{D}_i|$;
    $N_B = \lceil \frac{|\mathbb{D}_{\min}|}{|\mathcal{D}'|} N \rceil$;
    $\mathbb{B} \leftarrow$ uniformly sample N_B episodes from $\mathbb{D}_{\min}$;
    $\mathcal{B} \leftarrow \mathcal{B} \cup \mathbb{B}$;
    $\mathcal{D}' \leftarrow \mathcal{D}' \setminus \mathbb{D}_{\min}$;
    $N \leftarrow N - N_B$;
end while
Return $\mathcal{B}$

Algorithm 2. Diversified Experience Replay (DivER)

Parameters: MARL framework θ, target network $\theta^- = \theta$, representation model ϕ.

Initialize an empty replay buffer $\mathcal{D}$.
while *training* **do**
    for *episode* $\leftarrow 1$ **to** M **do**
        Initialize $\boldsymbol{E} = \emptyset$.
        for each time step t **do**
            for each agent k **do**
                Select an action based on the policy.
                Store the transition in $\boldsymbol{E}$.
            end for
            Calculate z_t with the representation model.
        end for
        Calculate the final representation z_T,
        Add the episodic data $\boldsymbol{E}$ and vector z_T to $\mathcal{D}$.
    end for
    Sample a mini-batch $\mathcal{B}$ according to Algorithm 1.
    Follow the MARL method to update θ,
    $\phi \leftarrow \phi + \lambda_\phi \nabla_\phi J_D$,
    Update z_T of each sample in $\mathcal{B}$ with new ϕ,
    Update target network $\theta^- \leftarrow \theta$ periodically,
    Update the cluster labels of all data in $\mathcal{D}$ periodically.
end while

4.4 Realization

Overall Learning Algorithm. The overall algorithm of DivER after integrating with the off-policy MARL framework is displayed in Algorithm 2. On the basis of the original MARL method, DivER only introduces an additional representation model during training and fully preserves the efficiency of the decision-making process. The parameter updates of the MARL framework and the representation model in DivER are independent and do not interfere with each other, enabling DivER to be easily integrated with different frameworks and achieve stable performance.

Hyperparameter Settings. The clustering algorithm and the number of clusters are two main hyperparameters for DivER. DivER employs the K-Means clustering algorithm by default in our implementation but is also compatible with various other algorithms such as DBSCAN [5] and Gaussian Mixture Models, and choosing a clustering algorithm that aligns with the true sample distribution can improve the effectiveness of DivER. A larger number of clusters requires higher computational costs but also leads to a smaller size for each cluster, which means a corresponding reduction in the coverage radius and improved sample diversity. For fairness, we set the number of clusters to 8 for algorithms that specify this hyperparameter, and employ the default hyperparameters for other algorithms.

5 Experiments

5.1 Experimental Setup

Environments. We select the most popular environment for MARL, StarCraft II Multi-Agent Challenges (SMAC) [27], as the main testbed to facilitate an intuitive comparison with previous off-policy MARL methods. SMAC contains two armies of units, and each ally is controlled by a decentralized agent that can only act based on its local observation while the enemy units are controlled by built-in handcrafted heuristic rules. To address SMAC's lack of stochasticity and get rid of open-loop policies, we further conduct experiments on the more challenging SMACv2 [3], which severely restricts the observability of agents and randomly initializes the scenarios. In our experiments, the difficulty level of built-in AI is set to 7 (very hard), and the version of StarCraft II engine is 4.6.2 instead of the simpler 4.10. Please note that results from different versions are not always comparable.

Baselines. The off-policy MARL baselines we selected can be categorized into three groups. QMIX [26] and QPLEX [37] are two recognized MARL frameworks that can be integrated with DivER. RODE [38] and LDSA [42] both modify the QMIX framework and promote multi-agent cooperation by increasing the diversity of agents' behaviors, achieving state-of-the-art (SOTA) performance. PER [28] is the most extensively studied and widely applied prioritized experience replay method, and we combine it with QMIX, denoted as QMIX-PER. To be consistent with the baselines, DivER is also combined with QMIX in our experiments unless otherwise specified. All baselines are implemented using the source codes in their original papers.

5.2 Experiment Results on SMAC

We present experiment results on 6 *Hard* and *Super Hard* SMAC scenarios in Fig. 4. The solid line represents the median win rates during training, with the 25–75% percentiles being shaded.

Although RODE and LDSA achieve higher win rates than DivER in *3s_vs_5z*, both of them promote multi-agent cooperation heuristically by increasing behavioral diversity of agents, leading to unstable performances across scenarios. Meanwhile, DivER focuses on sample diversity in the mini-batch, which can more broadly adapted to different scenarios. As we can see, DivER reaches the best performances in 4 out of all 6 scenarios with both the highest win rates and the earliest rise-ups, indicating its great sample efficiency. Since DivER is implemented on the basis of QMIX, we can observe that its performance significantly surpasses that of QMIX in all scenarios. Besides, DivER also outperforms the other prioritized experience replay method QMIX-PER. These evidences demonstrate the effectiveness and superiority of our proposed method.

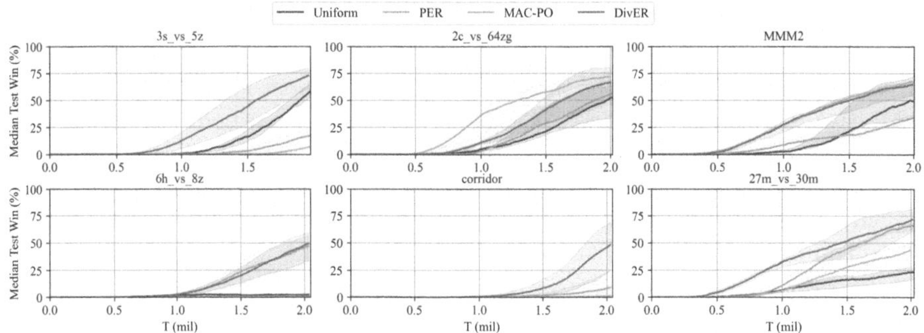

Fig. 4. Experiment results of DivER and baselines on SMAC.

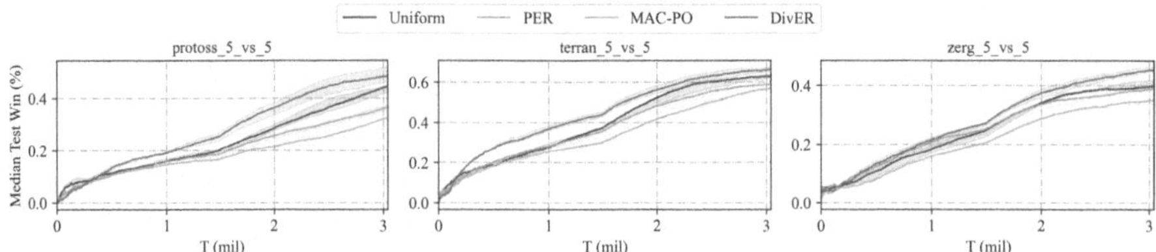

Fig. 5. Experiment results of DivER and baselines on SMACv2.

5.3 Experiment Results on SMACv2

[3] argue that the agent in SMAC may learn open-loop policy conditioned on the time step rather than the observation, thus can not adapt to diverse situations. Therefore, we further test DivER in the more random and difficult SMACv2 environment, and results are shown in Fig. 5. Meanwhile, PER sometimes even degrades the performance of QMIX, and methods based on behavioral diversity exhibit severe performance decline. Meanwhile, DivER makes stable improvements on the basis of QMIX, and its learning curves are positioned above and to the left of the baselines in all three scenarios. This suggests the high sample efficiency and stable performance of DivER, highlighting the broad effectiveness and great reliability of our diversity-based mini-batch sampling strategy.

We further extend the experiments on StarCraft II to ten million steps to evaluate DivER's convergence properties, and results can be found in Appendix D.

5.4 Ablation Study

In this subsection, we conduct ablation studies on two challenging *Super Hard* tasks, *MMM2* and *corridor*, to investigate following issues: (a) Can DivER be migrated to other frameworks? (b) Is DivER compatible with different clustering algorithms?

The Wide Applicability of DivER. As previously asserted, DivER can be integrated with any off-policy MARL framework. To better prove this claim, we further test the efficacy of integrating DivER with VDN [34] and Qatten [43] by comparing their performances with the original algorithms, and the results are in Fig. 6a. VDN is the simplest value-decomposition method and could not solve the two tasks at all, but its capability is significantly enhanced with the integration of DivER. In *MMM2*, DivER also significantly enhances the performance of Qatten. Meanwhile, although the final win rates of Qatten with and without DivER are very close in *corridor*, DivER still notably accelerates the learning process. This shows that DivER can be widely used in different MARL frameworks and maintain great effectiveness.

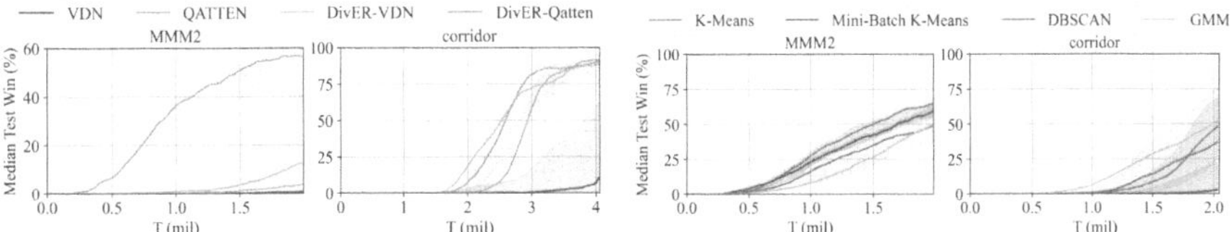

(a) The results of DivER integrated with other off-policy MARL methods.

(b) The performances of the variants of DivER employing different clustering algorithms.

Fig. 6. The results of DivER's variants for ablation studies.

Compatibility with Different Clustering Algorithms. As different clustering algorithms fit in different sample distributions and have distinct computational costs, DivER needs to be compatible with diverse algorithms to adapt to various tasks. Besides the default K-Means algorithm, we have also investigated Mini-Batch K-Means, DBSCAN, and Gaussian Mixture Models (GMM), and results are shown in Fig. 6b. While GMM is not suitable for the *MMM2* scenario, it exhibits the best performance in *corridor*. Mini-Batch K-Means enjoys high computational efficiency and performs close to K-Means in *MMM2*, but the inaccurate clustering also leads to failure in *corridor*. Therefore, choosing an appropriate clustering algorithm is of great importance for improving both the speed and performance of DivER.

6 Conclusion

Previous works have extensively investigated approaches to enhance off-policy MARL algorithms' performance, but few have considered the experience replay. Most related works still follow the prioritized experience replay techniques in the single-agent domain, which rank all experiences in the replay buffer based on their "importance scores" and select the most significant ones. In this work, we argue that a mini-batch with a higher sample diversity can help the model learn the relative advantage of different situations, thus accelerating the improvement of greedy policies. To this end, we propose a novel technique called **Div**ersified **E**xperience **R**eplay (DivER) to improve the sample diversity of the mini-batch in every training step. DivER first learns a representation model to embed the information of the entire sequence of states, based on which it then clusters the experiences in the replay buffer into groups and selects experiences proportionally from them for the mini-batch. This sample-diversity perspective demonstrates broad effectiveness across a variety of tasks. Besides, the workflow of DivER is independent of the MARL framework and does not affect the efficiency of agents' decision-making, making it a plug-and-play technique compatible with any off-policy MARL framework. We hope DivER can serve as a versatile and stable method for addressing general multi-agent tasks, as well as providing a new perspective for further research.

A Proofs

A.1 The Learning Target for DivER Model

Lemma 2. *The Equation below is a lower bound for mutual information* $\mathcal{I}(x_{t+1}, z_t)$*, and maximizing it leads to* $f(x_{t+1}, z_t)$ *approximating the density ratio in Eq. 4.*

$$\mathcal{J}_D = \sum_{i=1}^{N} \sum_{t=1}^{T-1} \log \frac{f(x_{t+1}^i, z_t^i)}{\sum_{j=1}^{N} f(x_{t+1}^j, z_t^j)}$$

Proof. This Equation can be viewed as the categorical cross-entropy of classifying the positive sample in contrastive learning, with $\frac{f}{\sum f}$ *being the predicted probability of the model. We rewrite the optimal probability as* $p(d=i|X_{t+1}, z_t^i)$ *with* $d=i$ *being the indicator that* x_{t+1}^i *is the positive sample, and* $X_{t+1} = \{x_{t+1}^1, ..., x_{t+1}^N\}$ *being the set of all encoded state at time* $t+1$ *in mini-batch* $\mathcal{B}$. *The probability that* x_{t+1}^i *was drawn from the conditional distribution* $p(x_{t+1}|z_t^i)$ *rather than the prior distribution* $p(x_{t+1})$ *can be derived as below:*

$$\begin{aligned} p(d=i|X, z_t^i) &= \frac{p(x_{t+1}^i|z_t^i)\prod_{x_{t+1}^k \in X_{t+1}\backslash\{x_{t+1}^i\}} p(x_{t+1}^k)}{\sum_{j=1}^N p(x_{t+1}^j|z_t^i)\prod_{x_{t+1}^k \in X_{t+1}\backslash\{x_{t+1}^i\}} p(x_{t+1}^k)} \\ &= \frac{\frac{p(x_{t+1}^i|z_t^i)}{p(x_{t+1}^i)}}{\sum_{j=1}^N \frac{p(x_{t+1}^j|z_t^i)}{p(x_{t+1}^j)}} \end{aligned}$$

According to the above results, the optimal value for $f(x_{t+1}^i, z_t^i)$ *in Eq. 6 is proportional to* $\frac{p(x_{t+1}^i|z_t)}{p(x_{t+1}^i)}$, *and is independent of the choice of the mini-batch size* N.

Since z_t *is a latent vector that assists in predicting* x_{t+1}, *the relation* $p(x_{t+1}|z_t) \geq p(x_{t+1})$ *holds. Replace the term* $f(x_{t+1}, z_t)$ *in* $\mathcal{J}_D$ *with* $\frac{p(x_{t+1}|z_t)}{p(x_{t+1})}$, *we have:*

$$\begin{aligned} \mathcal{J}_D &= \sum_{i=1}^{N}\sum_{t=1}^{T-1} \log\left[\frac{\frac{p(x_{t+1}^i|z_t^i)}{p(x_{t+1}^i)}}{\frac{p(x_{t+1}^i|z_t^i)}{p(x_{t+1}^i)} + \sum_{x_{t+1}^j \in X_{t+1}\backslash\{x_{t+1}^i\}} \frac{p(x_{t+1}^j|z_t^i)}{p(x_{t+1}^j)}}\right] \\ &= -\sum_{i=1}^{N}\sum_{t=1}^{T-1} \log\left[1 + \frac{p(x_{t+1}^i)}{p(x_{t+1}^i|z_t^i)} \sum_{x_{t+1}^j \in X_{t+1}\backslash\{x_{t+1}^i\}} \frac{p(x_{t+1}^j|z_t^i)}{p(x_{t+1}^j)}\right] \\ &\approx -\sum_{i=1}^{N}\sum_{t=1}^{T-1} \log\left[1 + \frac{p(x_{t+1}^i)}{p(x_{t+1}^i|z_t^i)}(N-1)\mathbb{E}_{x_{t+1}^j} \frac{p(x_{t+1}^j|z_t^i)}{p(x_{t+1}^j)}\right] \\ &= -\sum_{i=1}^{N}\sum_{t=1}^{T-1} \log\left[1 + \frac{p(x_{t+1}^i)}{p(x_{t+1}^i|z_t^i)}(N-1)\right] \\ &\leq -\sum_{i=1}^{N}\sum_{t=1}^{T-1} \log\left[\frac{p(x_{t+1}^i)}{p(x_{t+1}^i|z_t^i)}N\right] \\ &= \mathcal{I}(x_{t+1}, z_t) - \log N \end{aligned}$$

Therefore, $\mathcal{I}(x_{t+1}, z_t) \geq \log N + \mathcal{J}_D$, *which means* $\mathcal{J}_D$ *is a lower bound for mutual information* $\mathcal{I}(x_{t+1}, z_t)$. *It is worth noting that the inequality approximation in the above formula becomes more accurate as* N *increases, so increasing the mini-batch size is helpful for the training of DivER.*

A.2 The Improved Sample Diversity of DivER

Lemma 3. *Let $\mathcal{D}$ be a finite set of N points in a metric space (X, d). Let $\mathcal{B}$ be a mini-batch of b points sampled from $\mathcal{D}$. The coverage radius of $\mathcal{B}$ for $\mathcal{D}$ is $R(\mathcal{B}) = \sup_{y \in \mathcal{D}} \min_{x \in \mathcal{B}} d(y, x)$. We have $\mathbb{E}[R(\mathcal{B}_{div})] \leq \mathbb{E}[R(\mathcal{B}_{uni})]$, with strict inequality being typical.*

Notation:

- $\mathcal{B}_{uni}$: *A mini-batch of b points selected by random uniform sampling from $\mathcal{D}$.*
- $\mathcal{C} = \{C_1, \ldots, C_k\}$: *A partition of $\mathcal{D}$ into k non-empty clusters.*
- $N_j = |C_j|$: *The number of points in cluster C_j, so $\sum_{j=1}^{k} N_j = N$.*
- b_j: *The number of points sampled from cluster C_j in stratified sampling. Proportional allocation means $b_j \approx b \cdot (N_j/N)$. We assume $\sum_{j=1}^{k} b_j = b$.*
- $\mathcal{B}_{div}$: *A mini-batch formed by sampling b_j points from each C_j (typically uniformly at random within C_j).*

Proof. *Let $d_y(\mathcal{B}) = \min_{x \in \mathcal{B}} d(y, x)$. So $R(\mathcal{B}) = \max_{y \in \mathcal{D}} d_y(\mathcal{B})$. A direct proof of $E[\max d_y]$ is complex. Instead, we can argue using the concept of stochastic dominance or by considering the probability of a point being poorly covered. Let $F_{div}(r) = P(R(\mathcal{B}_{div}) \leq r)$ and $F_{uni}(r) = P(R(\mathcal{B}_{uni}) \leq r)$ be the cumulative distribution functions (CDFs) of the coverage radii. If $F_{div}(r) \geq F_{uni}(r)$ for all r (and strictly greater for some r), then R_{div} is stochastically smaller than R_{uni}, which implies $E[R_{div}] \leq E[R_{uni}]$.*

Consider any point $y \in \mathcal{D}$. Suppose $y \in C_j$. For stratified sampling (assuming $b_j \geq 1$ for the cluster C_j containing y): The b_j points sampled from C_j provide "local" coverage for points in C_j. The remaining $b - b_j$ points are sampled from other clusters. $P(d_y(\mathcal{B}_{div}) > r) = P($all b points in $\mathcal{B}_{div}$ are further than r from $y)$. Since b_j points are drawn from C_j, if r is larger than the effective radius of C_j achievable with b_j points, this probability becomes small.

For uniform random sampling: Let K_j be the (random) number of points in $\mathcal{B}_{uni}$ that are drawn from cluster C_j. K_j follows a hypergeometric distribution $H(N, N_j, b)$. The expectation $E[K_j] = b \cdot N_j/N \approx b_j$. However, K_j can be 0. $P(K_j = 0) = \frac{\binom{N-N_j}{b}}{\binom{N}{b}}$ if $b \leq N - N_j$. $P(d_y(\mathcal{B}_{uni}) > r) = \sum_{m=0}^{b_j^*} P(d_y(\mathcal{B}_{uni}) > r \mid K_j = m) P(K_j = m)$, where b_j^* is $\min(b, N_j)$. If $P(K_j = 0)$ is substantial (e.g., if C_j is small or b is small relative to N/N_j), and C_j is somewhat isolated from other clusters, then the term $P(d_y(\mathcal{B}_{uni}) > r \mid K_j = 0)$ can be large. This is because y must be covered by points sampled from $\mathcal{D} \setminus C_j$. Stratified sampling (assuming $b_j \geq 1$) ensures $K_j = b_j \geq 1$, eliminating the possibility of cluster C_j being entirely unrepresented in the sample (if it was chosen to receive samples). This directly reduces the probability that $y \in C_j$ is far from its closest point in $\mathcal{B}_{div}$.

More formally, $R(\mathcal{B}) = \max_{y \in \mathcal{D}} d_y(\mathcal{B})$. The uniform random sampling strategy allows for higher variability in the spatial dispersion of points in $\mathcal{B}_{uni}$. Some *realizations of $\mathcal{B}_{uni}$ will have points clustered in one region of $\mathcal{D}$, leaving other regions poorly covered, leading to a large $R(\mathcal{B}_{uni})$. Stratified sampling, by forcing b_j samples from each stratum C_j (for j where $b_j \geq 1$), ensures a degree of spatial representativeness. This limits the occurrence of very large values of $R(\mathcal{B}_{div})$. If a sampling strategy S_1 is more likely to produce "extreme" bad configurations than strategy S_2, then we expect $E[f(S_1)] \geq E[f(S_2)]$ if f measures the "badness". The set of points $\mathcal{D}$ can be thought of as a finite probability space where each point has mass $1/N$. The coverage radius $R(\mathcal{B})$ indicates how well the empirical measure induced by $\mathcal{B}$ covers the true measure of $\mathcal{D}$ in a geometric sense. Stratified sampling generally yields empirical measures that are "closer" (in various senses, like reduced variance for means) to the population measure. While a full proof of $F_{div}(r) \geq F_{uni}(r)$ is intricate for general cases, the intuition is that stratified sampling curtails the right tail of the distribution of $R(\mathcal{B})$ by preventing samples that are very poorly spread relative to the cluster structure. This leads to $E[R(\mathcal{B}_{div})] \leq E[R(\mathcal{B}_{uni})]$. Strict inequality typically holds if clustering is meaningful (strata differ in location/density) and uniform sampling has a non-negligible chance of missing or undersampling certain regions that stratified sampling covers by design.*

B Environment Details

B.1 SMAC

SMAC is a simulation environment for research in collaborative multi-agent reinforcement learning (MARL) based on Blizzard's StarCraft II RTS game. It provides various micro-battle scenarios and also supports customized scenarios for users to test the algorithms. The goal in each scenario is to control different types

Table 1. Information of selected challenges.

Challenge	Ally Units	Enemy Units	Type	Level of Difficulty
3s_vs_5z	3 Stalkers	5 Zealots	Homogeneous Asymmetric	Hard
2c_vs_64zg	2 Colossi	64 Zerglings	Homogeneous Asymmetric	Hard
MMM2	1 Medivac 2 Marauders 7 Marines	1 Medivac 3 Marauders 8 Marines	Heterogeneous Asymmetric	Super Hard
6h_vs_8z	6 Hydralisks	8 Zealots	Homogeneous Asymmetric	Super Hard
corridor	6 Zealots	24 Zerglings	Homogeneous Asymmetric	Super Hard
27m_vs_30m	27 Marines	30 Marines	Homogeneous Asymmetric	Super Hard

of ally agents to move or attack to defeat the enemies. The enemies are controlled by a heuristic built-in AI with adjustable difficulty level between 1 to 7. In our experiments, the difficulty of the game AI is set to the highest (the 7th level). The version of StarCraft II is 4.6.2 (B69232) in our experiments, and it should be noted that results from different client versions are not always comparable. Table 1 presents the details of selected scenarios in our experiments.

B.2 SMACv2

SMACv2 [3] is proposed to address SMAC's lack of stochasticity. In SMACv2, the sight range of the agents is narrowed, and the attack ranges of different unit types are no longer the same. The team compositions and agent start positions are generated randomly at the beginning of each episode. These modifications make SMACv2 extremely challenging. It is worth noting that the disparity between the lineups of the two sides can be substantial in some episodes due to the randomness in initialization. In these episodes, the outcomes are almost determined at the initialization stage but are little affected by the policies learned by the algorithms. We sifted out such episodes during testing to prevent blurring the gap between algorithms. The version of the StarCraft II engine is also 4.6.2 (B69232) in our experiments.

Table 2. The hyperparameter settings of DivER.

Description	Value
Type of value mixer	QMIX
Dimension of trajectory embedding	32
Dimension of hidden states in RNN	64
Dimension of the mixing network	32
Dimension of hypernetworks	64
Batch size	128
Trajectories sampled per run	4
Replay buffer size	2500
Discount factor γ	0.99
Probability of random action (ϵ)	1.0$\sim$0.05
Anneal time for ϵ	100000
Type of optimizer	Adam
Clustering algorithm	K-Means
Number of clusters	8
Learning rate for DivER	0.001
Learning rate for MARL framework	0.001
Target network update interval	200

C Implementation Details

C.1 Settings of Hyperparameters

We list the hyperparameters of the DivER in Table 2. The hyperparameters of the baselines in our experiments remain the same as their official implementations.

C.2 Experiments Compute Resources

We conducted our experiments on a platform with 2 Intel(R) Xeon(R) Platinum 8280 CPU 2.70GHz processors, each with 26 cores. Besides, we use a GeForce RTX 3090 GPU to facilitate the training procedure. The time of execution varies by scenario.

D Further Evaluation

To expedite the completion of numerous experiments and highlight DivER's superiority in sample efficiency, the experiments in the main text were conducted with two or three million steps. Here, we present the performances of DivER and all baselines after ten million steps (evaluated by the average value of the test win rates across 5 different random seeds), at which point the policies have undergone extensive updates and are mostly converged.

Table 3. Final performances of DivER and baselines

Scenarios	Difficulty	Off-policy Methods			
		Uniform	PER	MAC-PO	DivER
2c_vs_64zg	Hard	**100%**	**100%**	**100%**	**100%**
3s_vs_5z	Hard	98%	75%	66%	**100%**
8m_vs_9m	Hard	**100%**	**100%**	**100%**	**100%**
MMM2	Super Hard	98%	96%	**100%**	**100%**
5m_vs_6m	Hard	85%	88%	85%	**94%**
3s5z_vs_3s6z	Super Hard	75%	74%	80%	**86%**
6h_vs_8z	Super Hard	24%	**97%**	24%	96%
corridor	Super Hard	5%	94%	33%	**100%**
27m_vs_30m	Super Hard	**100%**	**100%**	**100%**	**100%**
protoss_5_vs_5		64%	54%	53%	**69%**
terran_5_vs_5		66%	64%	64%	**70%**
zerg_5_vs_5		49%	50%	47%	**62%**
Avg. Score (Hard+)		72%	82.7%	71%	**89.8%**

As shown in Table 3, DivER achieves the best convergence performance on a variety of scenarios. Therefore, DivER not only maintains its leading performance during the initial training phase, but also preserves its performance advantage after sufficient update steps, demonstrating its consistent superiority throughout the training horizon.

References

1. Ahilan, S., Dayan, P.: Correcting experience replay for multi-agent communication. arXiv preprint arXiv:2010.01192 (2020)
2. Brittain, M., Bertram, J., Yang, X., Wei, P.: Prioritized sequence experience replay. arXiv preprint arXiv:1905.12726 (2019)
3. Ellis, B., et al.: Smacv2: an improved benchmark for cooperative multi-agent reinforcement learning (2023)
4. Fan, S., Song, G., Yang, B., Jiang, X.: Prioritized experience replay in multi-actor-attention-critic for reinforcement learning. J. Phys: Conf. Ser. **1631**, 012040 (2020)
5. Fang-Ming, B., Wei-Kui, W., Long, C.: DBscan: Density-based spatial clustering of applications with noise. J. Nanjing Univ. (Natural Sci.) **48**(4), 491–498 (2012)
6. Gogineni, K., Wei, P., Lan, T., Venkataramani, G.: Scalability bottlenecks in multi-agent reinforcement learning systems. arXiv preprint arXiv:2302.05007 (2023)
7. Gu, S.: Safe multi-agent reinforcement learning for multi-robot control. Artif. Intell. **319**, 103905 (2023)
8. Gutmann, M., Hyvärinen, A.: Noise-contrastive estimation: a new estimation principle for unnormalized statistical models. In: Proceedings of the Thirteenth International Conference on Artificial Intelligence and Statistics, pp. 297–304. JMLR Workshop and Conference Proceedings (2010)
9. Iqbal, S., Sha, F.: Actor-attention-critic for multi-agent reinforcement learning (2019)
10. Jiang, A.H., et al.: Accelerating deep learning by focusing on the biggest losers. arXiv preprint arXiv:1910.00762 (2019)
11. Katharopoulos, A., Fleuret, F.: Not all samples are created equal: deep learning with importance sampling. In: International Conference on Machine Learning, pp. 2525–2534. PMLR (2018)
12. Lee, S.Y., Sungik, C., Chung, S.Y.: Sample-efficient deep reinforcement learning via episodic backward update. Adv. Neural Inf. Process. Syst. **32** (2019)
13. Lin, L.J.: Self-improving reactive agents based on reinforcement learning, planning and teaching. Mach. Learn. **8**, 293–321 (1992)
14. Liu, X.H.: Regret minimization experience replay in off-policy reinforcement learning. Adv. Neural. Inf. Process. Syst. **34**, 17604–17615 (2021)
15. Loshchilov, I., Hutter, F.: Online batch selection for faster training of neural networks. arXiv preprint arXiv:1511.06343 (2015)
16. Lowe, R., et al.: Multi-agent actor-critic for mixed cooperative-competitive environments. Adv. Neural Inf. Process. Syst. **30** (2017)
17. Mei, Y., Zhou, H., Lan, T.: Projection-optimal monotonic value function factorization in multi-agent reinforcement learning. In: AAMAS, pp. 2381–2383 (2024)
18. Mei, Y., Zhou, H., Lan, T., Venkataramani, G., Wei, P.: Mac-po: multi-agent experience replay via collective priority optimization. arXiv preprint arXiv:2302.10418 (2023)
19. Novati, G., Koumoutsakos, P.: Remember and forget for experience replay. In: International Conference on Machine Learning, pp. 4851–4860. PMLR (2019)
20. Oh, Y., Shin, J., Yang, E., Hwang, S.J.: Model-augmented prioritized experience replay. In: International Conference on Learning Representations (2022)

21. Oliehoek, F.A., Amato, C.: A concise introduction to decentralized POMDPs. Springer (2016)
22. Oord, A.v.d., Li, Y., Vinyals, O.: Representation learning with contrastive predictive coding. arXiv preprint arXiv:1807.03748 (2018)
23. Paul, M., Ganguli, S., Dziugaite, G.K.: Deep learning on a data diet: finding important examples early in training. Adv. Neural. Inf. Process. Syst. **34**, 20596–20607 (2021)
24. Pleiss, G., Zhang, T., Elenberg, E., Weinberger, K.Q.: Identifying mislabeled data using the area under the margin ranking. Adv. Neural. Inf. Process. Syst. **33**, 17044–17056 (2020)
25. Rashid, T., Farquhar, G., Peng, B., Whiteson, S.: Weighted QMIX: expanding monotonic value function factorisation for deep multi-agent reinforcement learning. Adv. Neural. Inf. Process. Syst. **33**, 10199–10210 (2020)
26. Rashid, T., et al.: QMIX: monotonic value function factorisation for deep multi-agent reinforcement learning. In: International Conference on Machine Learning, pp. 4295–4304. PMLR (2018)
27. Samvelyan, M., et al.: The starcraft multi-agent challenge. arXiv preprint arXiv:1902.04043 (2019)
28. Schaul, T.: Prioritized experience replay. arXiv preprint arXiv:1511.05952 (2015)
29. Sener, O., Savarese, S.: Active learning for convolutional neural networks: a core-set approach. arXiv preprint arXiv:1708.00489 (2017)
30. Shamsoshoara, A., Khaledi, M., Afghah, F., Razi, A., Ashdown, J.: Distributed cooperative spectrum sharing in UAV networks using multi-agent reinforcement learning. In: 2019 16th IEEE Annual Consumer Communications and Networking Conference (CCNC), pp. 1–6. IEEE (2019)
31. Son, K., Kim, D., Kang, W.J., Hostallero, D., Yi, Y.: QTRAN: learning to factorize with transformation for cooperative multi-agent reinforcement learning. CoRR **abs/1905.05408** (2019). http://arxiv.org/abs/1905.05408
32. Su, J., Adams, S., Beling, P.: Value-decomposition multi-agent actor-critics. In: Proceedings of the AAAI conference on artificial intelligence, vol. 35, pp. 11352–11360 (2021)
33. Sun, P., Zhou, W., Li, H.: Attentive experience replay. In: Proceedings of the AAAI Conference on Artificial Intelligence, vol. 34, pp. 5900–5907 (2020)
34. Sunehag, P., et al.: Value-decomposition networks for cooperative multi-agent learning. arXiv preprint arXiv:1706.05296 (2017)
35. Tampuu, A.: Multiagent cooperation and competition with deep reinforcement learning. PLoS ONE **12**(4), e0172395 (2017)
36. Tan, M.: Multi-agent reinforcement learning: independent vs. cooperative agents. In: Proceedings of the Tenth International Conference on Machine Learning, pp. 330–337 (1993)
37. Wang, J., Ren, Z., Liu, T., Yu, Y., Zhang, C.: QPLEX: Duplex Dueling Multi-Agent Q-Learning. arXiv preprint arXiv:2008.01062 (2020)
38. Wang, T., et al.: Rode: learning roles to decompose multi-agent tasks. arXiv preprint arXiv:2010.01523 (2020)
39. Wang, Y., Zhang, Z.: Experience selection in multi-agent deep reinforcement learning. In: 2019 IEEE 31st International Conference on Tools with Artificial Intelligence (ICTAI), pp. 864–870. IEEE (2019)
40. Wu, T., et al.: Multi-agent deep reinforcement learning for urban traffic light control in vehicular networks. IEEE Trans. Veh. Technol. **69**(8), 8243–8256 (2020)

41. Xu, Z., et al.: Multi-vehicle flocking control with deep deterministic policy gradient method. In: 2018 IEEE 14th International Conference on Control and Automation (ICCA), pp. 306–311. IEEE (2018)
42. Yang, M., et al.: LDSA: Learning dynamic subtask assignment in cooperative multi-agent reinforcement learning. Adv. Neural. Inf. Process. Syst. **35**, 1698–1710 (2022)
43. Yang, Y., et al.: Qatten: a general framework for cooperative multiagent reinforcement learning. arXiv preprint arXiv:2002.03939 (2020)
44. Zha, D., Lai, K.H., Zhou, K., Hu, X.: Experience replay optimization. arXiv preprint arXiv:1906.08387 (2019)
45. Zhang, Z., Han, S., Wang, J., Miao, F.: Spatial-temporal-aware safe multi-agent reinforcement learning of connected autonomous vehicles in challenging scenarios. In: 2023 IEEE International Conference on Robotics and Automation (ICRA), pp. 5574–5580. IEEE (2023)

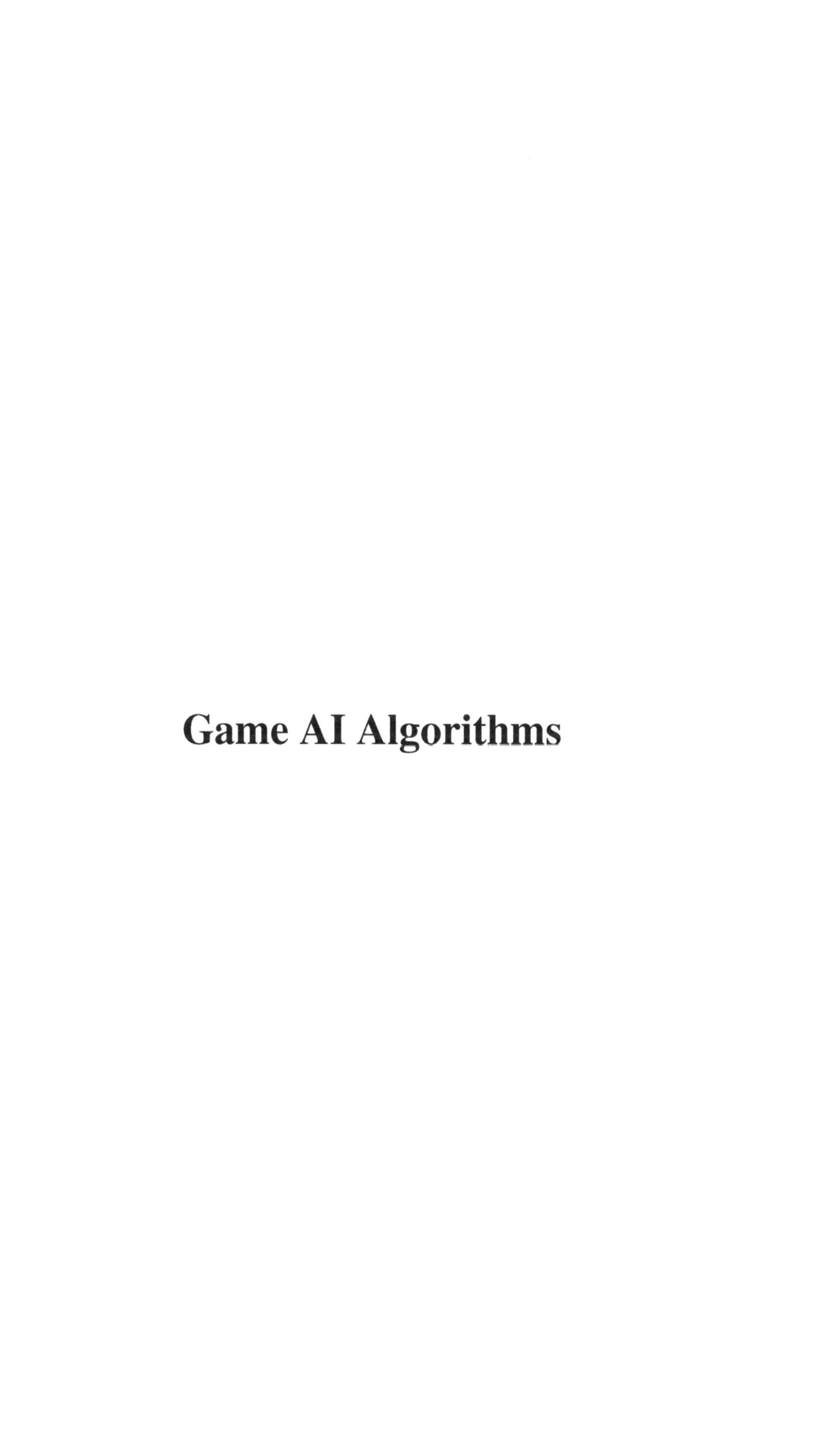

Game AI Algorithms

Making Mahjong Agents Interpretable: A Parameterized Search Approach

Lingfeng Li, Yunlong Lu, Yongyi Wang, Qifan Zheng, and Wenxin Li(✉)

Peking University, Beijing, China
lwx@pku.edu.cn

Abstract. People need to internalize the skills of AI agents to improve their own capabilities. Our paper focuses on Mahjong, a multiplayer game involving imperfect information and requiring effective long-term decision-making amidst randomness and hidden information. Through the efforts of AI researchers, several impressive Mahjong AI agents have already achieved performance levels comparable to those of professional human players; however, these agents are often treated as black boxes from which few insights can be gleaned. This paper introduces Mxplainer, a parameterized search algorithm that can be converted into an equivalent neural network to learn the parameters of black-box agents. Experiments conducted on AI and human player data demonstrate that the learned parameters provide human-understandable insights into these agents' characteristics and play styles. In addition to analyzing the learned parameters, we also showcase how our search-based framework can locally explain the decision-making processes of black-box agents for most Mahjong game states.

Keywords: Explainable AI · Card Games · Machine Learning

1 Introduction

Games play a pivotal role in the field of AI, offering unique challenges to the research community and serving as fertile ground for the development of novel AI algorithms. Board games, such as Go [23] and chess [22], provide ideal settings for perfect-information scenarios, where all agents are fully aware of the environment states. Card games, like heads-up no-limit hold'em (HUNL) [5,6], Doudizhu [29,30], and Mahjong [11], present different dynamics with their imperfect-information nature, where agents must infer and cope with hidden information from states. Video games, such as Starcraft [26], Minecraft [7], and Honor of Kings [27], push AI algorithms to process and extract crucial features from a multitude of signals amidst noise.

Conversely, the advancement of AI algorithms also incites new enthusiasm in games. The work of AlphaGo [21] in 2016 has had a long-lasting impact on the Go community. It revolutionized the play style of Go, a game with millennia of history, and changed the perspectives of world champions on this game [28].

J. Haqbeen et al. (Eds.): IJCAI 2025, LNAI 16400, pp. 107–125, 2026.
https://doi.org/10.1007/978-981-95-9667-6_8

Teaching tools based on AlphaGo [8] have become invaluable resources for newcomers while empowering professional players to set new records [18].

Mahjong, a worldwide popular game with unique characteristics, has gained traction in the AI research community as a new testbed. It brings its own flavor as a multiplayer imperfect-information environment. First, there is no rank of individual tiles in Mahjong; all tiles are equal in their role within the game. A game of Mahjong is not won by beating other players in card ranks but by being the first to reach a winning pattern. Therefore, state evaluation is more challenging for Mahjong players, as they need to assess the similarity and distance between game states and the closest game goals. Second, the game objective in Mahjong is to become the first to complete one of many possible winning patterns. The optimal goal can frequently change when players draw new tiles during gameplay. In fact, Mahjong's core difficulty lies in selecting the most effective goal among numerous possibilities. Players must evaluate their goals and make decisions upon drawing each tile and reacting to other players' discarded tiles. This decision-making process often involves situations where multiple goals are of similar distance, requiring trade-offs that distinguish play styles and reveal a player's level of expertise.

Several strong agents have already been developed for different variants of Mahjong rules [10,11,32]. Without the use of explainable AI methods [2,12], people can only observe the agents' actions without understanding how the game states are evaluated or which game goals are preferred that lead to those actions.

In Explainable AI (XAI) [3], black-box models typically refer to neural networks that lack inherent transparency and thus rely on post-hoc explanation tools for interpretability [12]. Current post-hoc XAI tools, such as Grad-CAM [20] and LIME [17], are primarily designed for neural networks. While these tools can explain how input features affect outputs, they do not provide insights into agents' decision-making processes.

In this paper, we present Mxplainer (**M**ahjong E**xplainer**), a parameterized classical agent framework designed to serve as an analytical tool for explaining the decision-making process of black-box Mahjong agents. Specifically, we have developed a parameterized framework that forms the basis for a family of search-based Mahjong agents. This framework is then translated into an equivalent neural network model, which can be trained using gradient descent to mimic any black-box Mahjong agent. Finally, the learned parameters are used to populate the parameterized search-based agents. We consider these classical agents to be inherently explainable because each calculation and decision step within them is comprehensible to human experts. This enables detailed interpretation and analysis of the decision-making processes and characteristics of the original black-box agents.

Through a series of experiments on game data from both AI agents and human players, we demonstrate that the learned parameters effectively reflect the decision processes of agents, including their preferred game goals and tiles to play. Our research also shows that by delving into the framework components, we can interpret the decision-making process behind the actions of black-box agents.

This paper pioneers research on analyzing Mahjong agents by presenting Mxplainer, a framework to explain black-box decision-making agents using search-based algorithms. Mxplainer allows AI researchers to profile and compare both AI agents and human players effectively. Additionally, we propose a method to convert any parameterized classical agent into a neural agent for automatic parameter tuning.

2 Related Works

In Explainable AI (XAI) [3] is a research domain dedicated to developing techniques for interpreting AI models for humans. This field encompasses several categories: classification models, generative AI, and decision-making agents. A specific subfield within this domain is Explainable Reinforcement Learning (XRL) [15], which focuses on explaining the behavior of decision-making agents. Explanations in XRL can be classified into two main categories: global and local.

Global explanations provide a high-level perspective on the characteristics and overall strategies of black-box agents, answering questions such as how an agent's strategy differs from others. Local explanations, on the other hand, focus on the detailed decision-making processes of agents, elucidating why an agent selects action A over B under specific scenarios.

XRL methods can be classified into intrinsic and post-hoc methods. Intrinsic methods directly generate explanations from the original black-box models, while post-hoc methods rely on additional models to explain existing ones. Imitation Learning (IL) [1,19] is a family of post-hoc techniques that approximate a target policy. LMUT [13] constructs a U-tree with linear models as leaf nodes and approximates target policies through a node-splitting algorithm and gradient descent. Q-BSP [9] uses batched Q-value to partition nodes and generate trees efficiently. EFS [31] employs an ensemble of linear models with non-linear features generated by genetic programming to approximate target policies. These methods have been tested and excelled in environments such as CartPole, MountainCar, and others in the Gym [4]. However, they rely on properly sampled state-action pairs to generate policies and may not be robust to out-of-distribution (OOD) states, which is particularly crucial for Mahjong with its high-dimensional state space and imperfect information.

PIRL [25] distinguishes itself among IL methods by introducing parameterized policy templates using its proposed policy programming language. It approximates the target π through fitting parameters with Bayesian Optimization in Markov games, achieving high performance in the TORCS car racing game. Compared to TORCS, Mahjong has far more complex state features and requires encoding action histories within states to obtain the Markov property. Additionally, Mahjong agents must make multi-step decisions from game goal selection to tile picking. Similar to PIRL, we define a parameterized search-based framework and optimize parameters using batched gradient descent to address these challenges.

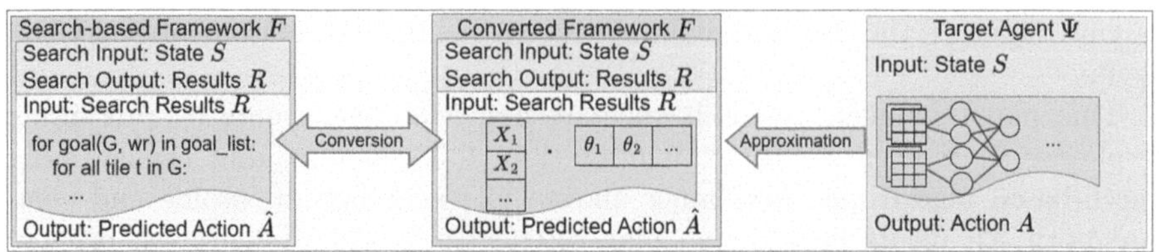

Fig. 1. The overview of Mxplainer. Search-based Framework F is a manually-engineered, domain-specific, parameterized template. A component of F can be converted into an equivalent network for supervised learning, where parameters of F serve as neurons. Target agents Ψ are black-box agents to be analyzed, and they can be approximated by the converted F.

3 Methods

We first introduce the general concepts of Mxplainer and then present the details of the implementations in the following subsections. To facilitate readability, we use uppercase symbols to indicate concepts, and lowercase symbols with subscripts for instances of concepts.

Figure 1 presents the concept overview of Mxplainer. We assume that the search-based nature of F is explainable to experts in the domain, such as Mahjong players and researchers. Within F, there are parameters Θ that control the behaviors of F. To explain a specific target agent Ψ, we would like the behaviors of F to approximate those of Ψ as closely as possible. In order to automate and speed up the approximation process, we convert a part of F that contains Θ into an equivalent neural network representation, and leverage supervised learning to achieve the goals.

F consists of Search Component SC and Calculation Component CC, denoted as $F = SC|CC$. SC searches and proposes valid goals in a fixed order. Next, CC takes groups of manually defined parameters Θ, each of which carries meanings and is explainable to experts, and makes decisions based on the search results from SC, as shown in Fig. 2.

CC can be converted into an equivalent neural network N, whose neurons are semantically equivalent to Θ. $SC|N$ can approximate any target agents Ψ by fitting Ψ's state-action pairs. Since Θ is the same for both CC and N, learned $\hat{\Theta}$ can be put back into CC and explains actions locally through step-by-step deductions of $SC|CC$. Moreover, by normalizing and studying Θ, Mxplainer is able to compare and analyze agents' strategies and characteristics.

The construction of F and the design of parameters Θ are problem-related, as they reflect researchers' and players' attention to the game's characteristics and the game agents' strategies. The conversion from CC to N and the approximation through supervised learning is problem agnostic and can be automated. Out of Mxplainer, SC of F is fixed and the same for all agents, but behaviors of CC and N change as Θ changes for different target agents Ψ.

3.1 Parameters Θ of Framework F

For Θ, we manually craft three groups of parameters to model people's general understanding of Mahjong, Θ_{tile}, Θ_{fan}, and Θ_{meld}.

Θ_{tile} is used to break ties between tiles, and different players may have different preferences for tiles.

Θ_{fan} is designed to break ties between goals when multiple goals are equally distant from the current hand. There are more than billions of possible goals in Mahjong, but each goal consists of **fans**. Thus, we use the compound of preferences of **fans** to sort goals. We hypothesize that there exists a natural order of difficulty between **fans**, which implies that some are more likely to achieve than others. However, such an order is impossible to obtain unless there is an oracle that always gives the best action. Additionally, players break ties based on their inclinations towards **fans**. Since the natural difficulty order and players' inclinations are hard to decouple, we use Θ_{fan} to represent their products. Consequently, Θ_{fan} between different **fans** for a single player cannot be compared directly, but Θ_{fan} for the same **fans** between different players reflect their comparative preferences.

Θ_{meld} are the linear weights of a heuristic function that approximates the probability of **melding** a tile from other players. The linear function takes features from local game states, including the number of total unshown tiles, the length of game steps, and the unshown tile counts of the neighboring tiles. The components and the usage of Θ_{meld} will be discussed in detail in the following sections.

3.2 Search Component SC of Framework F

In Mahjong, **Redundant Tiles** R refer to the tiles in a player's hand that are considered useless for achieving their game goals. In contrast, **Missing Tiles** M are the ones that players need to acquire in future rounds to complete their objectives. Following that, **Shanten Distance** is defined as $D = |M|$, which conveys the distance between the current hand and a selected goal.

Here, we define a game goal as $G = (M, R, \Phi)$, since when both M and R are fixed, a game goal is set, and its corresponding **fans** Φ can be calculated. Each tile $t \in M$ additionally has two indicators, i_p and i_c, which determine if it can be acquired through melding from other players. i_p is true if the player already owns two tiles in the **Pung**, and the same happens to i_c and **Chow**. Thus, $\forall t \in M$, it has (t, i_p, i_c).

Through dynamic programming, we can efficiently propose different combinations of tiles and test if they satisfy MCR's winning condition. We can search all possible goals, but not all goals are reasonable to be considered as candidates. In practice, only up to 64 goals G are returned in ascending **Shanten Distances** D, since in most cases, only the closest goals are important to decisions, and they are usually less than two dozen.

However, only goals are not enough. MCR players also need to consider other observable game information to jointly evaluate the win rate of each goal G, such

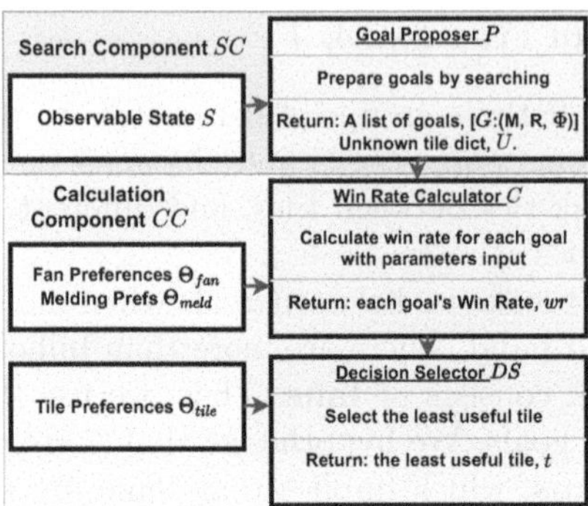

Fig. 2. Components of Framework F. Search Component SC uses Goal Proposer P for goal search. Calculation Component CC consists of Win Rate Calculator C and Decision Selector DS, and it is responsible for action calculations. The least useful tile t can be considered as the tile that appears least frequently among the most probable goals. Consequently, removing this tile has the least impact on the expected win rate.

as other players' discard history and unshown tiles. For our framework F, we only consider unshown tiles U, a dictionary keeping track of the number of each tile that is not shown through observable information.

Thus, the Goal Proposer P accepts game state information S, and outputs $([G], U)$, such that $0 < |[G]| \leq 64$, as shown in Fig. 2-A. In most cases, goals G in $[G]$ can be split into several groups. Different groups contain different **fans** Φ and represent different paths to win, while the goals within each group have different tile combinations for the same **fans** Φ.

3.3 Calculation Component CC of Framework F

Calculation Component CC of Framework F consists of Win Rate Calculator C and Decision Selector DS. CC contains three groups of tunable parameters Θ_{fan}, Θ_{meld}, and Θ_{tile} that control the behavior of Win Rate Calculator C and Decision Selector DS. In all, these three groups of parameters, Θ_{fan}, Θ_{meld}, and Θ_{tile}, are similar to parameters of neural networks, and they are the key factors that control the behaviors of agents derived from framework F.

The Win Rate Calculator C takes the results of the Goal Proposer P, $([G], U)$ as input and estimates the win rate for each goal G. The detailed algorithm of C is shown in Algorithm 1. Simply put, C multiplies the probability of successfully collecting each **missing tile** of a proposed goal as its estimated win rate.

The estimation of win rate in Win Rate Calculator C depends on the two groups of parameters, Θ_{fan} and Θ_{meld}. The probability of acquiring each tile is made of two parts: drawing by oneself or **melding** another player's discarded tile. For each tile t[1], we model the probability of drawing it as $P(t) = U[t]/Z$, in which $Z = sum(U)$. We assume the tile is drawn uniformly from all unshown tiles. The

[1] t represents a generic tile. $t \in X$ refers to a tile in collection X.

second part of the probability is partly determined by Θ_{meld}, representing agents' optimism of forming **melds**.

As discussed previously, Θ_{meld} is the parameter for a heuristic function that takes in local game features. The features are $\{Z, \frac{1}{Z}, 1-\frac{1}{Z}, L, \frac{1}{L}, 1\text{-}\frac{1}{L}, U[t-2] : U[t+2], bias\}$, where Z is the number of total unshown tiles, L is the length of game, and $U[t-2] : U[t+2]$ represents the unshown counts of adjacent tiles centered around the tile t. With an additional bias term, Θ_{meld} represents 12 linear weights in total.

For simplicity, uniform distribution is used to estimate the probability of collecting tiles because we designed the learned parameters only to reflect the characteristics of the agents' play styles. On the other hand, tie-breaking between multiple goals with similar **shanten numbers** frequently happens in Mahjong. Players break ties by leaning towards their preferred **fans**, and such preferences are captured by Θ_{fan}. Thus, in Θ_{fan}, a higher value of weight for a specific **fan** represents a higher preference of the agent for this **fan**.

The Decision Selector DS collects results from the Win Rate Calculator C and calculates the final action based on each goal's estimated win rates. The detailed algorithm for S is shown in Algorithm 2. The goal of S is to efficiently select the tile to discard with the most negligible impact on the overall win rate. Heuristically, the required tiles of goals with higher win rates are more important than those with lower ones. Conversely, the **redundant tiles** of such goals are more worthless since their existence actually hinders the goals' completion. Thus, each tile's worthless degree can be computed by accumulating the win rate of goals that regard it as a **redundant tile**, and the tile with the highest worthless degree has the most negligible impact on the overall win rate. Decision Selector DS accepts Θ_{tile} as parameters, which are used similarly as Θ_{fan} to break ties between tiles. For action predictions, such as **Chow** or **Pung**, F records win rates computed by C, assuming those actions are taken, and F selects the action with the highest win rate.

3.4 Differentiable Network N of Mxplainer

The Search-based Framework F is a parameterized search-based agent template, and its parameters Θ need to be tuned to approximate any target agents' behaviors. Luckily, Calculator C and Decision Selector DS only contain fixed-limit loops, with each iteration independent from others and if-else statements whose outcomes can be pre-computed in advance. Thus, C and S can be converted into an equivalent neural network N for parallel computation, and the parameters Θ can be optimized through batched gradient descent. The rules for the conversion can be found in Appendix B.

The Resulting Network N and the Training Objective. The sizes and meanings of the network N outputs and three groups of parameters are reported in Table 1.

The learning objectives depend on the form of target agents Ψ and the problem context. Since we are modeling the selection of actions as classification problems, we use cross entropy (CE) loss between the output of N and the label Y.

Table 1. Sizes and meanings of Neural Network N's components. Action **Pung** becomes **Kong** if **Kong** is possible

Entry	Size	Meaning
Overall Output	39	Combined output size
Output (Action)	5	5 Actions:
		Pass, 3 types of **Chow**, **Pung**
Param Θ_{fan}	80	Preference for all 80 **fans**
Params Θ_{meld}	12	Linear features weights w/ bias
Param Θ_{tile}	34	Preference for all 34 tiles

The label can be soft or hard depending on whether the target agent gives probability distributions. Since we cannot access human players' action distribution, we use actions as hard ground-truth labels for all target agents. Additionally, an L2-regularization term of $(\Theta_{fan} - abs(\Theta_{fan}))^2$ is added to penalize negative values of **fan** preferences to make the heuristic parameters more reasonable.

After supervised training, the learned parameters Θ can be directly filled back into CC. Since CC is equivalent to N, $SC|CC(\Theta)$ inherits the characteristics of $SC|N(\Theta)$, approximating the target agent Ψ. By analyzing the parameterized agent $SC|CC(\Theta)$, we can study the parameters to learn the comparative characteristics between agents and gain insights into the deduction process of Ψ through the step-by-step algorithms of Framework $SC|CC$. Since only data pairs are required from the target agents, we can use Mxplainer on both target AI agents and human players.

4 Experiments

We conducted a series of experiments to evaluate the effectiveness of Mxplainer in generating interpretable models and analyze their explainability. Three different target agents are used in these experiments. The first agent ψ_1 is a search-based MCR agent with manually specified characteristics as a baseline. Specifically, this agent only considers the **fan** of *Seven Pairs* to choose, and all its actions are designed to reach this target as efficiently as possible. When multiple tiles are equally good to discard, a fixed order is predefined to break the equality. The second agent ψ_2 is the strongest MCR AI from an online game AI platform, Botzone [33]. The third agent ψ_3 is a human MCR player from an online Mahjong platform, MahjongSoft.

Around 8,000 and 50,000 games of self-play data are generated for the two AI agents. Around 34,000 games of publicly available data are collected from the game website for the single human player over more than 3 years. Through supervised learning on these datasets, three sets of parameters $\theta_{1,2,3}$ are learned and filled back in the Search-based Framework F as-is, making interpretable white-box agents $\hat{\psi}_{1,2,3}$ with similar behavior to the target agents $\psi_{1,2,3}$. The weights for each agent are selected with the highest validation accuracy from

Table 2. A). Defined Order for tiles and their learned weights. B). Sorted weights in the learned parameters $\theta_{1,fan}$ and their corresponding **fans**. Learned weights for $\theta_{2,fan}$ are added for comparison. C). The **major fans** of ψ_2 and ψ_3 with a difference of at least 1% in historical frequency, which is calculated from their game history data.

A	Tile Name	Defined Order	$\theta_{1,tile}$
	White Dragon	1	1.41
	Green Dragon	2	1.13
	Red Dragon	3	1.07
B	**Fan** Name	$\theta_{1,fan}$	$\theta_{2,fan}$
	Seven Pairs	56.19	3.59
	Pure Terminal Chows	7.42	1.99
	Four Pure Shift Pungs	4.10	0.42
C	**Fan** Name	Frequency Diff $\psi_2 - \psi_3(\%)$	Param Diff $\theta_{2,fan} - \theta_{3,fan}$
	Pure Straight	1.30	0.45
	Mixed Straight	1.94	0.65
	Mixed Triple Chow	2.09	0.63
	Half Flush	1.04	0.27
	Mixed Shifted Chows	5.08	0.31
	All Types	2.60	0.27
	Melded Hand	-8.25	-1.24
	Fully Concealed Hand	1.83	-0.55

three runs. To make weights comparable across different agents, reported weights are normalized with $100 * (\Theta - \Theta_{min})/\Sigma(\Theta - \Theta_{min})$.

Since it is common in MCR where multiple **redundant tiles** can be discarded in any order, it is difficult to achieve high top-1 accuracy on the validation sets, especially for ψ_2 and ψ_3, which have no preference on the order of tiles to discard. As a reference of the similarity, $\hat{\psi}_{1,2,3}$ achieves top-3 accuracy of 97.15%, 92.75%, 90.12% on the data of $\psi_{1,2,3}$.

4.1 Correlation Between Behaviors and Parameters

In the Search-based Framework F, the parameters Θ are designed to be strategy-related features that should take different values for different target agents. Here we analyze the correlation between the learned parameters and target agents' behavior to prove that Mxplainer can extract high-level characteristics of agents and explain their behavior.

Preference of **fans** *to choose* Θ_{fan} stands for the relative preference of agents to win by choosing each **fan**. For the baseline target ψ_1 which only chooses the **fan** of *Seven Pairs*, the top values of $\theta_{1,fan}$ learned are shown in Table 2-B. We also include $\theta_{2,fan}$ values for comparisons, demonstrating the differences in learned weights between specialized *Seven Pairs* agent and other agents. It can be seen that the weight for *Seven Pairs* is much higher than those of other **fans**, showing the strong preference of $\hat{\psi}_1$ to this **fan**. The **fans** with the second and third largest weights are patterns similar to *Seven Pairs*, indicating $\hat{\psi}_1$ also tends to approach them during the gameplay based on its learned action choices, though it eventually ends with *Seven Pairs* for 100% of the games. For targets ψ_2 and ψ_3 with unknown preferences of **fans**, we count the frequency of occurrences of each **major fan** in their winning hands as an implication of their preferences and compare these two agents on both the frequency and the learned weights of each **fan**. Table 2-C shows all the **major fans** with a difference of 1% in frequency. Except for the last row, the data shows a significant positive correlation between the preference of target agents ψ and the learned θ_{fan}.

Preference of tiles to discard Θ_{tile} stands for the relative preference of discarding each tile, especially when multiple **redundant tiles** are valued similarly. Since ψ_2 and ψ_3 show no apparent preference in discarding tiles, we focus on the analysis of ψ_1, which is constructed with a fixed tile preference. We find the learned weights almost form a monotonic sequence with only three exceptions out of 34 tiles, showing strong correlation between the learned parameters and the tile preferences of the target agent. Table 2-A shows the first a few entries of $\theta_{1,tile}$.

4.2 Manipulation of Behaviors by Parameters

Previous experiments have shown that greater frequencies of **fans** within the game's historical record lead to elevated preferences. In this experiment, we illustrate that through the artificial augmentation of **fan** preferences, the modified agents, in contrast, display elevated frequencies of the corresponding **fans**. We make adjustments to the parameters $\theta_{2,fan}$ within $\hat{\psi}_2$ by multiplying the weight assigned to the *All Types* fan by a factor of 10. This gives rise to the generation of a new agent, ψ_2', which is expected to exhibit a stronger inclination towards selecting this **fan**.

We collect roughly around 8,000 self-play game data samples from ψ_2 and ψ_2'. Subsequently, we determine the frequency with which each fan shows up in their winning hands. The data indicates that among all the fans, only the *All Types* fan undergoes a frequency variation that surpasses 1%. Its frequency has risen from 2.59% to 5.76%, signifying an increment of 3.17%. In contrast, the frequencies of all other **major fans** have experienced changes of less than 1%. Given that Mahjong is a game characterized by a high level of randomness in both the tile-dealing and tile-drawing processes, adjusting the parameters related to fan preferences can only bring about a reasonable alteration in the actual behavior patterns of the target agents. In conjunction with the findings of previous experiments, we can draw the conclusion that the parameters within Mxplainer are, in fact, significantly correlated with the behaviors of agents. Moreover, through the

Table 3. A). An example game state at the beginning of the game where no tiles have been discarded by other players. B). Some proposed goals for state s by $\hat{\psi}_2$ and the estimated win rate. "H&K" is an abbreviation for *Honors and Knitted* due to space constraint.

A	Other Known Information			Current Hand
	None			
B ID	**Major Fan**	Win Rate	**Redundant Tiles** R	Final Target
25	*Lesser H&K Tiles*[1]	1.000	D7, C9, B6, B8, B9	
0	*Knitted Straight*[1]	0.125	C9, B9, NW, RD, WD	
11	*Pure Straight*	0.018	D2, C3, C6, NW, RD, WD	
50	Seven Pairs[1]	0.017	B6, B8, B9, NW, RD, WD	

analysis of these parameters, we are capable of discerning the agents' preferences and high-level behavioral characteristics.

4.3 Interpretation of Deduction Process

In this subsection, we analyze the deduction process of the Search-based Framework F on an example game state by tracing the intermediate results of $\hat{\psi}_2$ to demonstrate the local explainability of Mxplainer agents in decision-making.

The selected game state S is at the beginning of a game with no tiles discarded yet, and the player needs to choose one to discard, as shown in Table 3-A. The target black-box agent ψ_2, selects the tile B9 as the optimal choice to discard for unknown reasons. However, analyses of the execution of the white-box agent $\hat{\psi}_2$ explain the choice.

The Search Component SC proposed 64 possible goals for s, and Table 3-B shows a few goals representative of different **major fans**. With fitted θ_2, Algorithm 1 produces an estimated win rate for each goal G, as listed under the "Win Rate" column of Table 3-B. We observe that though B9 is required in goals such as *Pure Straight*, it is not required for many goals with higher estimated win rates, such as *Knitted Straight*[2].

Following Algorithm 2, we accumulate the win rates for tiles in **Redundant Tiles** R. A higher value of a tile indicates a higher win rate if the tile is discarded, and B9 turns out to have a higher value than other tiles by a large margin, which is consistent with the observed decision of ψ_2.

This section merely demonstrates an analysis of action selection within the context of a simple Mahjong state. However, such analyses can be readily extended to other complex states. The Search Component SC consistently takes in information and puts forward the top 64 reachable goals, ranked according to distances. The Calculation Component CC calculates the win rate for each goal using the learned parameters. Finally, an action is chosen based on these win rates.

[2] A **fan** that do not follow the pattern of four melds and a pair.

Without Mxplainer, people can only observe the actions of black-box MahJong agents, but cannot understand how the decisions are made. Our experiments show that Mxplainer's fitted parameters can well approximate and mimic target agents' behaviors. By examining the fitted parameters and Mxplainer's calculation processes, experts are able to interpret the considerations of black-box agents leading to their actions.

5 Discussion

With Mxplainer, we can compare the differences between agents. By comparing the fitted parameters in parallel with other agents, we can analyze the characteristics of different agents. For example, we can easily observe that the black-box AI agent ψ_2 has a much higher weight on *Thirteen Orphans*, *Seven Pairs*, and *Lesser H&K Tiles*. In contrast, the human player ψ_3 has a significant inclination of making *Melded Hand*, and these observations are indeed backed by their historical wins in Supplemental Material B.

Our proposed approach has a unique advantage in quantifying and tuning weights for custom-defined task-related features in areas where interpretability and performance are crucial. While Mxplainer is specifically designed for Mahjong, we hypothesize that its unique approach and XAI techniques may be applicable to other applications. In fact, we experimentally applied our proposed framework to two examples: Mountain Car from Gym [4] and Blackjack [24]. Both examples, which can be found in Appendix I, confirmed the effectiveness of our proposed method. However, the scope of application of our method still requires further study.

6 Conclusion

In summary, with Mxplainer, we construct, convert, and train domain-specific classical agents with hand-crafted parameters to interpret black-box agents. Our experiments show that Mxplainer can learn meaningful characteristics of Mahjong agents and locally interpret agents' decisions with excellent transparency. Of the three steps in Mxplainer, only the construction of the classical agent is task-related, and the conversion and the training steps can be automated. We hypothesize that this explanation template can be generalized to other problems, and we plan to extend our method for general classical agents and other applications in the future.

A Mounter Car and Black Jack

In Mountain Car, the observation space is location **L** and speed **S**, both of which can be positive or negative. The action space are accelerations to the left or right. We can design a heuristic template H which takes the sign of **L** and **S** as input, and the heuristics Θ are actions for these four states. The Transformation T

is also simple: we map **L** and **S** to the four states during data processing and output an one-hot mask for Θ. When imitating the optimal strategy, the learned Θ can be found in Fig. 3-A, which also achieves optimal control.

In Blackjack, the observation space includes usable ace **A**, dealer's first card **C**, and player's sum of points **S**. The action space is to hit or stick under each state. The Heuristic Template H is designed to act based on heuristic boundaries Θ of **S** for Hit or Stick for each (**A**, **C**) pair. The Transformation T is again mapping (**A**, **C**) pairs to their masks, respectively. The optimal strategy and the learned Θ is shown in Fig. 3-B, showing that the framework learns exactly the same behavior with the target model i.e. the optimal strategy.

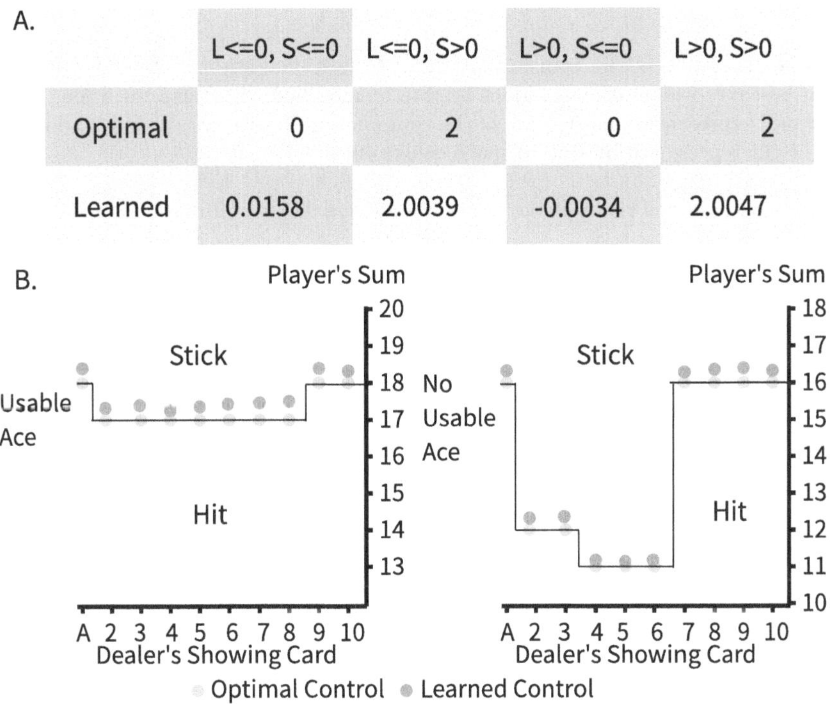

A.

	L<=0, S<=0	L<=0, S>0	L>0, S<=0	L>0, S>0
Optimal	0	2	0	2
Learned	0.0158	2.0039	-0.0034	2.0047

Fig. 3. Optimal Parameters and Learned Parameters for A) Mountain Car and B) Black Jack.

B Rules and Examples of Transformation of Non-differential Structures

Boolean-to-Arithmetic Masking (M) is defined as a one-hot vector of dim $|n|$ for a conditional statement with n branches. If a conditional branch can be determined without parameters, M can be computed and stored as input data; otherwise, M can be computed at runtime. Computations for results R are the same for all branches, but only one result is activated through $R \cdot M$.

Padding Value (P) is defined as the identity element of its related operator. Identity elements ensure that any computation paths with P produce no-op results, and they are required for the treatment of loops. For example, if the results of a loop are gathered through a summation operation, then the computation path with P produces 0. If the results are gathered through multiplication, then the path with P produces 1. This is because for classical agents to be optimized and parallelized, loops must be set with upper limits, similar to the maximum sequence length when training a recurrent neural network. P needs to fill the iterations where there is no actual data. To keep the Framework F exactly the same as the transformed network N, all upper limits of loops need to be reflected in the original loops of F. Table 4 summarizes M and P.

Table 4. Examples of the transformation for Conditional statements and loops. Note that classical representations of loops need to be modified with the same upper limit as the neural representations. $V^{\top[1,2]}$ is the example input with axis 1 and 2 transposed for efficient representation due to space constraints.

Conditional	Classical Representation	Neural Representation (Pytorch)

	`def foo(a,b):`
	`    if P:`
	`        r = a*3+b*4`
	`        return r`
	`    elif Q:`
	`        return a*b`
	`    else`
	`        return a/b`
		`def forward(A, B, M):`
		`    p = A*3 + B*4`
		`    q = A*B`
		`    o = A/B`
		`    out = torch.cat([p,q,o], dim=1)`
		`    return torch.sum(out*M, dim=1)`

Loop A	Classical Representation	Neural Representation (Pytorch)

Note: Results are independent between Iterations.	`def bar1(A):`
	`    res = []`
	`    e = enumerate`
	`    for i,a in e(A):`
	`        if i>64:`
	`            break`
	`        r = 2*(a+1)`
	`        res.append(r)`
	`    p = np.prod`
	`    return p(res)`
		`def forward(V):`
		`    V1 = V.view(n*64, 2)`
		`    O = V1[:,0]*2*(V1[:,1]+1)`
		`    # convert padding values to 1`
		`    # for the final torch.prod()`
		`    O += 1-V1[:, 0]`
		`    O1 = O.view(n, 64)`
		`    return torch.prod(O1, dim=1)`

Loop B	Classical Representation	Neural Representation (Pytorch)

Note: Results are dependent between Iterations.	`def bar2(A):`
	`    res = []`
	`    e = enumerate`
	`    for i,a in e(A):`
	`        if i>64:`
	`            break`
	`        r=a`
	`        if i!=0:`
	`            r += res[-1]`
	`        res.append(r)`
	`    return sum(res)`
		`def forward(V):`
		`    res = []`
		`    for i in range(64):`
		`        if i==0:`
		`            r = V[:, i, 1]`
		`        else:`
		`            # computing real data`
		`            r = res[-1]+V[:, i, 1]`
		`        # set zero for padding values`
		`        r*=V[:, i, 0]`
		`        res.append(r)`
		`    res = torch.stack(res)`
		`    res = torch.sum(res, dim=0)`
		`    return res`

C Mahjong the Game

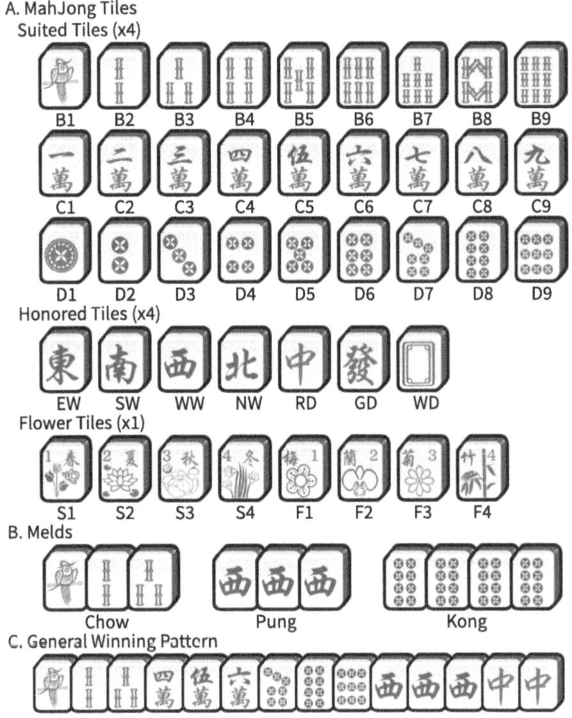

Fig. 4. Basics of Mahjong. A). All the Mahjong tiles. There are four identical copies for suited tiles and honored tiles, and one copy for each flower tile. B). Examples of Chow, Pung, and Kong. Note that only suited tiles are available for Chow. C). Example of the general winning pattern.

Mahjong is a four-player imperfect information tile-based tabletop game. The complexity of imperfect-information games can be measured by information sets, which are game states that players cannot distinguish from their own observations. The average size of information sets in Mahjong is around 10^{48}, making it a much more complex game to solve than Heads-Up Texas Hold'em [14], whose average size of information sets is around 10^3. To facilitate the readability of this paper, we highlight terminologies used in Mahjong with **bold texts**, and we distinguish scoring patterns (**fans**) by *italicized texts*.

In Mahjong, there are a maximum of 144 tiles, as shown in Fig. 4-A. Despite its plethora of rule variants, Mahjong's general rules are the same. On a broad level, Mahjong is a pattern-matching game. Each player begins with 13 tiles only observable to themselves, and they take turns to draw and discard one tile until one completes a game goal with a 14th tile. The general pattern of 14 tiles is four

melds and a pair, as shown in Fig. 4-C. A meld can take the form of **Chow**, **Pung**, and **Kong**, as shown in Fig. 4-B. Apart from drawing all the tiles by themselves, players can take the tile just discarded by another player instead of drawing one to form a **meld**, called **melding**, or declare a win.

C.1 Official International Mahjong

Official International Mahjong stipulates Mahjong Competition Rules (MCR) to enhance the game's complexity and competitiveness and weaken its gambling nature. It specifies 80 scoring patterns with different points, called "**fan**", ranging from 1 to 88 points. In addition to the winning patterns of four melds and a pair, players must have at least 8 points by matching multiple scoring patterns to declare a win.

Specific rules and requirements for each pattern can be found in this book [16]. Of 81 **fans**, 56 are highly valued and called **major fans** since most winning hands usually consist of at least one. The standard strategy of MCR players is to make game plans by identifying several **major fans** closest to their initial set of tiles. Then, depending on their incoming tiles, they gradually select one of them as the terminal goal and strive to collect all the remaining tiles before others do. The exact rules of MCR are detailed in *Official International Mahjong: A New Playground for AI Research* [14].

D Algorithms

Algorithm 1. Win Rate Estimation for A Single Goal

Input: Goal G: < **missing tiles** M:< t, **Chow** indicator i_c, **Pung** indicator i_p>, **fan** list F >, unshown dict U, game length L
Parameter: Θ_{fan}, Θ_{meld}
Output: Estimated win rate for goal G

```
Initialize win rate wr ← 100
for all missing tile m ∈ M do
    // Construct local tile feature x_m from game length L,
    // and remaining adjacent tile count U.
    x_m ← U, L
    // Calculate prob. of drawing m and others discarding m
    p_draw ← U[m]/sum(U)
    p_discard ← U[m]/sum(U) * Θ_meld * x_m
    source ← 0
    if i_p then
        source ← 3 // one can pung from all others
    else if i_c then
        source ← 1 // one can only chow from the one left
    end if
    p_meld ← p_discard * source
    wr ← wr × (p_draw + p_meld)
end for
Total fan weight fw ← ∑ Θ_fan[f] for fan f ∈ F
wr ← wr × fw
return wr
```

Algorithm 2. Discarding Tile Selection

Input: List of goals and their win rates $L = [(\text{Goal } G, \text{Win rate } wr)]$, Hand tiles H
Parameter: Θ_{tile}
Output: Tile to discard

Initialize tile values $d \leftarrow$ Dict $\{\text{tile } t : 0\}$
for all $(G, wr) \in L$ **do**
  for all tile $t \in G$ **do**
    $d[t] \leftarrow d[t] + wr$ // **redundant tiles**
  end for
end for
for all tile $t \in d$ **do**
  $d[t] \leftarrow d[t] \times \Theta_{tile}[t]$
end for
return $\arg\max_{t \in H} d[t]$

References

1. Abbeel, P., Ng, A.: Apprenticeship learning via inverse reinforcement learning. In: Proceedings of the Twenty-first International Conference on Machine Learning (2004). https://api.semanticscholar.org/CorpusID:207155342
2. Arrieta, A.B., et al.: Explainable artificial intelligence (XAI): concepts, taxonomies, opportunities and challenges toward responsible ai (2019)
3. Barredo Arrieta, A., et al.: Explainable artificial intelligence (XAI): concepts, taxonomies, opportunities and challenges toward responsible ai. Inf. Fusion **58**, 82–115 (2020).https://doi.org/10.1016/j.inffus.2019.12.012. https://www.sciencedirect.com/science/article/pii/S1566253519308103
4. Brockman, G., et al.: Openai gym (2016)
5. Brown, N., Sandholm, T.: Superhuman ai for heads-up no-limit poker: libratus beats top professionals. Science **359**(6374), 418–424 (2018). https://doi.org/10.1126/science.aao1733.
6. Brown, N., Sandholm, T.: Superhuman ai for multiplayer poker. Science **365**(6456), 885–890 (2019). https://doi.org/10.1126/science.aay2400. https://www.science.org/doi/abs/10.1126/science.aay2400
7. Fan, L., et al.: Minedojo: building open-ended embodied agents with internet-scale knowledge (2022)
8. Huang, A., Hui, F., Baker, L.: Alphago teach (2017). https://alphagoteach.deepmind.com/. Accessed 12 Apr 2024
9. Jhunjhunwala, A., Lee, J., Sedwards, S., Abdelzad, V., Czarnecki, K.: Improved policy extraction via online q-value distillation. In: 2020 International Joint Conference on Neural Networks (IJCNN), pp. 1–8 (2020). https://doi.org/10.1109/IJCNN48605.2020.9207648
10. Li, J., Wu, S., Fu, H., Fu, Q., Zhao, E., Xing, J.: Speedup training artificial intelligence for mahjong via reward variance reduction. In: 2022 IEEE Conference on Games (CoG), pp. 345–352. IEEE Press (2022). https://doi.org/10.1109/CoG51982.2022.9893584
11. Li, J., et al.: Suphx: mastering mahjong with deep reinforcement learning (2020)

12. Linardatos, P., Papastefanopoulos, V., Kotsiantis, S.: Explainable ai: a review of machine learning interpretability methods. Entropy **23**(1) (2021).https://doi.org/10.3390/e23010018. https://www.mdpi.com/1099-4300/23/1/18
13. Liu, G., Schulte, O., Zhu, W., Li, Q.: Toward interpretable deep reinforcement learning with linear model u-trees. In: Berlingerio, M., Bonchi, F., Gärtner, T., Hurley, N., Ifrim, G. (eds.) Machine Learning and Knowledge Discovery in Databases, pp. 414–429. Springer International Publishing, Cham (2019)
14. Lu, Y., Li, W., Li, W.: Official international mahjong: a new playground for ai research. Algorithms **16**(5) (2023). https://doi.org/10.3390/a16050235. https://www.mdpi.com/1999-4893/16/5/235
15. Milani, S., Topin, N., Veloso, M., Fang, F.: Explainable reinforcement learning: a survey and comparative review. ACM Comput. Surv. **56**(7) (2024). https://doi.org/10.1145/3616864
16. Novikov, V.: Handbook on mahjong competition rules (2016). http://mahjongeurope.org/portal/images/docs/mcr_EN.pdf. Accessed 17 July 2023
17. Ribeiro, M.T., Singh, S., Guestrin, C.: why should I trust you?: Explaining the predictions of any classifier. CoRR **abs/1602.04938** (2016). http://arxiv.org/abs/1602.04938
18. Saedol, L.: 8 years later: a world go champion's reflections on alphago (2024). https://blog.google/around-the-globe/google-asia/8-years-later-a-world-go-champions-reflections-on-alphago/. Accessed 12 Apr 2024
19. Schaal, S.: Is imitation learning the route to humanoid robots? Trends Cogn. Sci. **3**(6), 233–242 (1999). https://doi.org/10.1016/S1364-6613(99)01327-3. https://www.sciencedirect.com/science/article/pii/S1364661399013273
20. Selvaraju, R.R., Das, A., Vedantam, R., Cogswell, M., Parikh, D., Batra, D.: Grad-cam: why did you say that? visual explanations from deep networks via gradient-based localization. CoRR **abs/1610.02391** (2016). http://arxiv.org/abs/1610.02391
21. Silver, D., et al.: Mastering the game of go with deep neural networks and tree search. Nature **529**(7587), 484–489 (2016). https://doi.org/10.1038/nature16961
22. Silver, D., et al.: Mastering chess and shogi by self-play with a general reinforcement learning algorithm (2017)
23. Silver, D., et al.: Mastering the game of go without human knowledge. Nature **550**(7676), 354–359 (2017). https://doi.org/10.1038/nature24270
24. Sutton, R.S., Barto, A.G.: Reinforcement learning: an introduction. A Bradford Book, Cambridge, MA, USA (2018)
25. Verma, A., Murali, V., Singh, R., Kohli, P., Chaudhuri, S.: Programmatically interpretable reinforcement learning. In: Dy, J., Krause, A. (eds.) Proceedings of the 35th International Conference on Machine Learning. Proceedings of Machine Learning Research, vol. 80, pp. 5045–5054. PMLR (10–15 Jul 2018). https://proceedings.mlr.press/v80/verma18a.html
26. Vinyals, O., et al.: Grandmaster level in starcraft ii using multi-agent reinforcement learning. Nature **575**(7782), 350–354 (2019). https://doi.org/10.1038/s41586-019-1724-z
27. Wei, H., et al.: Honor of kings arena: an environment for generalization in competitive reinforcement learning (2022)
28. Willingham, E.: Ai's victories in go inspire better human game playing (2023). https://www.scientificamerican.com/article/ais-victories-in-go-inspire-better-human-game-playing/. Accessed 12 Apr 2024
29. Yang, G., et al.: Perfectdou: dominating doudizhu with perfect information distillation (2024)

30. Zha, D., et al.: Douzero: mastering doudizhu with self-play deep reinforcement learning (2021)
31. Zhang, H., Zhou, A., Lin, X.: Interpretable policy derivation for reinforcement learning based on evolutionary feature synthesis. Complex Intell. Syst. **6**(3), 741–753 (2020). https://doi.org/10.1007/s40747-020-00175-y
32. Zhao, X., Holden, S.B.: Building a 3-player mahjong ai using deep reinforcement learning (2022)
33. Zhou, H., Zhang, H., Zhou, Y., Wang, X., Li, W.: Botzone: An online multi-agent competitive platform for ai education. In: Proceedings of the 23rd Annual ACM Conference on Innovation and Technology in Computer Science Education, pp. 33–38. ITiCSE 2018, Association for Computing Machinery, New York, NY, USA (2018). https://doi.org/10.1145/3197091.3197099

Author Index

J. Haqbeen et al. (Eds.): IJCAI 2025, LNAI 16400, p. 127, 2026.
https://doi.org/10.1007/978-981-95-9667-6

The manufacturer's authorised representative in the EU is Springer Nature Customer Service Centre GmbH, Europaplatz 3, 69115 Heidelberg, Germany. If you have any concerns regarding our products, please contact ProductSafety@springernature.com

Printed and bound by CPI Group (UK) Ltd, Croydon, CR0 4YY

15/07/2026

02167587-0001